Geneviève Behrend

Awaken the Inner Power

e-artnow 2022

Geneviève Behrend
Awaken the Inner Power

Your Invisible Power, How to Live Life and Love it, Attaining Your Heart's Desire

e-artnow, 2022
Contact: info@e-artnow.org

ISBN 978-80-273-4525-0

Contents

Your Invisible Power 13

FOREWORD 14

Chapter 1: ORDER OF VISUALIZATION 16

Chapter 2: HOW TO ATTRACT TO YOURSELF THE THINGS YOU DESIRE 18

Chapter 3: RELATION BETWEEN MENTAL AND PHYSICAL FORM 20

Chapter 4: OPERATION OF YOUR MENTAL PICTURE 21

Chapter 5: EXPRESSIONS FROM BEGINNERS 25

Chapter 6: SUGGESTIONS FOR MAKING YOUR MENTAL PICTURE 27

Chapter 7: THINGS TO REMEMBER 28

Chapter 8: WHY I TOOK UP THE STUDY OF MENTAL SCIENCE 29

Chapter 9: HOW I ATTRACTED TO MYSELF TWENTY THOUSAND DOL-LARS 31

Chapter 10: HOW I BECAME THE ONLY PERSONAL PUPIL OF THE GREATEST MENTAL SCIENTIST OF THE PRESENT DAY 34

Chapter 11: HOW TO BRING THE POWER IN YOUR WORD INTO ACTION 38

Chapter 12: HOW TO INCREASE YOUR FAITH 39

Chapter 13: THE REWARD OF INCREASED FAITH 40

Chapter 14: HOW TO MAKE NATURE RESPOND TO YOU 41

Chapter 15: FAITH WITH WORKS – WHAT IT HAS ACCOMPLISHED 42

Chapter 16: SUGGESTIONS AS TO HOW TO PRAY OR ASK, BELIEVING YOU HAVE ALREADY RECEIVED 44

Chapter 17: THINGS TO REMEMBER 50

How to Live Life and Love it 51

Foreword 52

Chapter 1: LIVE LIFE AND LOVE IT! 53

Chapter 2: THE FINE ART OF GIVING 57

Chapter 3: THE ART OF RECIPROCITY 60

Chapter 4: GOD-CONSCIOUSNESS VERSUS SENSE-CONSCIOUSNESS 64

Chapter 5: PERSONAL INTIMACY WITH GOD 69

Chapter 6: INDIVIDUALITY 74

Chapter 7: PERSONAL POINTERS ON SUCCESS 78

Chapter 8: INSTANTANEOUS HEALING 83

Chapter 9: INSTANTANEOUS HEALING (Cont'd) 87

Chapter 10: IS DESIRE A DIVINE IMPULSE? 92

Chapter 11: IS DESIRE A DIVINE IMPULSE? 97

Chapter 12: EXERCISES FOR HEALTH 105

Chapter 13: "HOW TO LIVE LIFE AND LOVE IT!" 109

Chapter 14: IMAGINATION AND INTUITION 112

Chapter 15: HUSBANDS, WIVES, CHILDREN AND WILLS 115

Chapter 16: LIFE, LOVE, BEAUTY 119

Attaining Your Heart's Desire 123

Foreword 124

Judge Thomas T. Troward, Philosopher and Sage 126

Lesson I: Interpreting the Word 133

Lesson II: How to Get What you Want 153

Lesson III: How to Overcome Adverse Conditions 167

Lesson IV: Strengthening Your Will 182

Lesson V: Making Your Subjective Mind Work for You 190

Lesson VI: Hourly Helps 206

Lesson VII: Putting Your Lessons into Practice 221

Your Invisible Power

FOREWORD

These pages have been written with purpose and hope that their suggestions may furnish you a key to open up the way to the attainment of your desires, and to explain that Fear should be entirely banished from your effort to obtain possession of the things you desire. This presupposes, of course, that your desire for possession is based upon your aspiration for greater liberty. For example, you feel that the possession of more money, lands or friends will make you happier, and your desire for possession of these things arises from a conviction that their possession will bring you liberty and happiness.

In your effort to possess you will discover that the thing you most and ultimately need is to "Be," always (not spasmodically) your best self -that self which understands that the mistakes of those you love are simply misunderstandings. Your feeling that greater possessions, no matter of what kind they may be, will, of themselves bring you contentment or happiness, is a misunderstanding. No person, place or thing can give you happiness. They may give you cause for happiness and a feeling of contentment, but the joy of Living comes from within. Therefore, it is here recommended, rather than otherwise, that you should make the effort to obtain the things which you feel will bring you joy, provided, as previously stated, that your desires are in accord with the joy of Living.

It is also desired, in this volume, to suggest the possibilities in store for all who make persistent effort to understand the Law of Visualization and make practical application of this knowledge on whatever plane he or she may be. The word "effort," as here employed, is not intended to convey the idea of strain. All study and meditation should be without strain or tension.

It has been my endeavor to show that by starting at the beginning of the creative action or the mental picture, certain corresponding results are sure to follow. "While the laws of the Universe cannot be altered, they can be made to work under specific conditions, thereby producing results for individual advancement which cannot be obtained under the spontaneous working of the law provided by Nature."

However far the suggestions I have given you of the possibilities in store for you through visualizing may carry you beyond your past experience, they nowhere break the continuity of the law of cause and effect.

If through the suggestions here given anyone is brought to realize that their mind is a center through and in which "all power there is" is in operation, simply waiting to be given direction in the one and only way through which it can take specific action (and this means reaction in concrete or physical form), then the mission to which this book is dedicated has been fulfilled.

Try to remember that the picture you think, feel and see is reflected into the Universal Mind, and by the natural law of reciprocal action must return to you in either spiritual or physical form. Knowledge of this law of reciprocal action between the individual and the Universal Mind opens to you free access to all you may wish to possess or to be.

It must be steadfastly borne in mind that all this can only be true for the individual who recognizes that they derive their power to make an abiding mental picture from the All-Originating Universal Spirit of Life (God), and can be used constructively only so long as it is employed and retained in harmony with the Nature of the Spirit which originated it. To insure this there must be no inversion of the thought of the individual regarding their relationship to this Universal Originating Spirit which is that of a son or daughter, through which the parent mind acts and reacts.

Thus conditioned, whatever you think and feel yourself to be; the Creative Spirit of Life is bound to faithfully reproduce in a corresponding reaction. This is the great reason for picturing yourself and your affairs as you wish them to be as existing facts (though invisible to the physical eye), and live in your picture. An honest endeavor to do this, always recognizing that your own mind is a projection of the Originating Spirit, will prove to you that the best there is, is yours in all your ways.

Chapter 1

ORDER OF VISUALIZATION

The exercise of the visualizing faculty keeps your mind in order, and attracts to you the things you need to make life more enjoyable in an orderly way. If you train yourself in practice of deliberately picturing your desire and carefully examining it, you will soon find your thought and desires come and proceed in more orderly procession than ever before. Having reached a state of ordered mentality you are no longer in a constant state of mental hurry. Hurry is Fear and consequently destructive.

In other words, when your understanding grasps the power to visualize your heart's desire and hold it with your will, it attracts to you all things requisite to the fulfillment of that picture by the harmonious vibrations of the law of attraction. You realize that since Order is Heaven's first law, and visualization places things in their natural element, then it must be a heavenly thing to visualize.

Everyone visualizes, whether they know it or not. Visualizing is the great secret of Success. The conscious use of this great power attracts to you greatly multiplied resources, intensifies your wisdom, and enables you to make use of advantages which you formerly failed to recognize.

We now fly through the air, not because anyone has been able to change the laws of Nature, but because the inventor of the flying machine learned how to apply Nature's laws and, by making orderly use of them, produced the desired result. So far as natural forces are concerned, nothing has changed since the beginning. There were no airplanes in "the Year One," because those of that generation could not conceive the idea as a practical working possibility. "It has not yet been done" was the argument, "and it cannot be done." Yet the laws and materials for practical flying machines existed then as now.

Troward tells us that the great lesson he learned from the airplane and wireless telegraphy is the triumph of principle over precedent, and the working of an idea to its logical conclusion in spite of accumulated testimony of all past experience.

With such an example before you, can you not realize that still greater secrets may be disclosed? Also "That you hold the key within yourself, with which to unlock the secret chamber that contains your heart's desire? All that is necessary in order that you may use this key and make your life exactly what you wish it to be, is a careful inquiry into the unseen causes which stand back of every external and visible condition. Then bring these unseen causes into harmony with your conception, and you will find that you can make practical working realities of possibilities which at present seem but fantastic dreams."

We all know that the balloon was the forefather of the airplane. In 1766 Henry Cavendish, an English nobleman, proved that hydrogen gas was seven times lighter than atmospheric air. From that discovery the balloon came into existence, and from the ordinary balloon the dirigible, a cigar-shaped airship, was evolved. Study of aeronautics and the laws of aerial locomotion of birds and projectiles led to the belief that mechanism could be evolved by which heavier-than-air machines could be made to travel from place to place and remain in the air by the maintenance of great speed which would overcome by propulsive force the ordinary law of gravitation.

Professor Langley of Washington who developed much of the theory which others afterward improved was subjected to much derision when he sent a model airplane up only to have it bury its nose in the muddy water of the Potomac. But the Wright Brothers, who experimented in the latter part of the Nineteenth Century, realized the possibility of traveling through the air in a machine that had no gas bag. They saw themselves enjoying this mode of transportation with great facility. It is said that one of the brothers would tell the other (when their varied experiments did not turn out as they expected): "It's all right, brother, I can see myself riding in that machine, and it travels easily and steadily." Those Wright Brothers knew what they wanted, and kept their pictures constantly before them.

In visualizing, or making a mental picture, you are not endeavoring to change the laws of Nature. You are fulfilling them. Your object in visualizing is to bring things into regular order both mentally and physically. When you realize that this method of employing the creative power brings your desires, one after another, into practical material accomplishment, your confidence in the mysterious but unfailing law of attraction, which has its central power station in the very heart of your word/picture, becomes supreme. Nothing can shake it. You never feel that it is necessary to take anything from anybody else. You have learned that asking and seeking have receiving and finding as their correlatives. You know that all you have to do is to start the plastic substance of the Universe flowing into the thought-molds your picture-desire provides.

Chapter 2

HOW TO ATTRACT TO YOURSELF THE THINGS YOU DESIRE

The power within you which enables you to form a thought picture is the starting point of all there is. In its original state it is the undifferentiated formless substance of life. Your thought picture forms the mould (so to speak) into which this formless substance takes shape. Visualizing, or mentally seeing things and conditions as you wish them to be, is the condensing, the specializing power in you that might be illustrated by the lens of a magic lantern. The magic lantern is one of the best symbols of this imaging faculty. It illustrates the working of the Creative Spirit on the plane of the initiative and selection (or in its concentrated specializing form) in a remarkably clear manner.

This picture slide illustrates your own mental picture -invisible in the lantern of your mind until you turn on the light of your will. That is to say, you light up your desire with absolute faith that the Creative Spirit of Life, in you, is doing the work. By the steady flow of light of the will on the Spirit, your desired picture is projected upon the screen of the physical world, an exact reproduction of the pictured slide in your mind.

Visualizing without a will sufficiently steady to inhibit every thought and feeling contrary to your picture would be as useless as a magic lantern without the light. On the other hand, if your will is sufficiently developed to hold your picture in thought and feeling, without any "ifs," simply realizing that your thought is the great attracting power, then your mental picture is as certain to be projected upon the screen of your physical world as any pictured slide put into the best magic lantern ever made.

Try projecting the picture in a magic lantern with a light that is constantly shifting from one side to the other, and you will have the effect of an uncertain will. It is as necessary that you should always stand back of your picture with a strong, steady will, as it is to have a strong steady light back of a picture slide.

The joyous assurance with which you make your picture is the very powerful magnet of Faith, and nothing can obliterate it. You are happier than you ever were, because you have learned to know where your source of supply is, and you rely upon its never-failing response to your given direction.

When all said and done, happiness is the one thing which every human being wants, and the study of visualization enables you to get more out of life than you ever enjoyed before. Increasing possibilities keep opening out, more and more, before you.

A business man once told me that since practicing visualization and forming the habit of devoting a few minutes each day to thinking about his work as he desired it to be in a large, broad way, his business had more than doubled in six months. His method was to go into a room every morning before breakfast and take a mental inventory of his business as he had left it the evening before, and then enlarge upon it. He said he expanded and expanded in this way until his affairs were in remarkably successful condition. He would see himself in his office doing everything that he wanted done. His occupation required him to meet many strangers every day. In his mental picture he saw himself meeting these people, understanding their needs and supplying them in just the way they wished. This habit, he said, had strengthened and steadied his will in an almost inconceivable manner. Furthermore, by thus mentally seeing things as he wished them to be, he had acquired the confident feeling that a certain creative power was exercising itself, for him and through him, for the purpose of improving his little world.

When you first begin to visualize seriously, you may feel, as many others do, that someone else may be forming the same picture you are, and that naturally would not suit your purpose. Do not give yourself any unnecessary concern about this. Simply try to realize that your picture is an orderly exercise of the Universal Creative Power specifically applied. Then you may be sure that no one can work in opposition to you. The universal law of harmony prevents this.

Endeavor to bear in mind that your mental picture is Universal Mind exercising its inherent powers of initiative and selection specifically.

God, or Universal Mind, made man for the special purpose of differentiating Himself through him. Everything that is, came into existence in this same way, by this self-same law of self-differentiation, and for the same purpose. First the idea, the mental picture or the prototype of the thing, which is the thing itself in its incipiency or plastic form.

The Great Architect of the Universe contemplated Himself as manifesting through His polar opposite, matter, and the idea expanded and projected itself until we have a world -many worlds.

Many people ask, "But why should we have a physical world at all?" The answer is: Because it is the nature of originating substance to solidify, under directivity rather than activity, just as it is the nature of wax to harden when it becomes cold, or plaster of paris to become firm and solid when exposed to the air. Your picture in this same Divine substance in its fluent state taking shape through the individualized center of Divine operation, your mind; and there is no power to prevent this combination of spiritual substance from becoming physical form. It is the nature of Spirit to complete its work and an idea is not complete until it has made for itself a vehicle.

Nothing can prevent your picture from coming into concrete form except the same power that gave it birth -yourself. Suppose you wish to have a more orderly room. You look about your room and the idea of order suggests boxes, closets, shelves, hooks and so forth. The box, the closet, the hooks, all are concrete ideas of order. Vehicles through which order and harmony suggest themselves.

Chapter 3

RELATION BETWEEN MENTAL AND PHYSICAL FORM

Some persons feel that it is not quite proper to visualize for things. "It's too material" they say. But material form is necessary for the self-recognition of spirit from the individual standpoint. And this is the means through which the creative process is carried forward. Therefore, far from matter being an illusion and something that ought not to be (as some metaphysical teachers have taught), matter is the necessary channel for the self-differentiation of spirit. However, it is not my desire to lead you into lengthy and tiresome scientific reasoning in order to remove the mystery of visualization and to put it upon a logical foundation. Naturally, each individual will do this in his own way. My only wish is to point out to you the smoothest way I know, which is the road on which Troward guides me. I feel sure you will conclude as I have, that the only mystery in connection with visualizing is the mystery of life taking form, governed by unchangeable and easily understood laws.

We all possess more power and greater possibilities than we realize, and visualizing is one of the greatest of these powers. It brings other possibilities to our observation. When we pause to think for a moment, we realize that for a cosmos to exist at all, it must be the outcome of a cosmic mind, which binds "all individual minds to a certain generic unities of action, thereby producing all things as realities and nothing as illusions." If you will take this thought of Troward's and meditate upon it without prejudice, you will surely realize that concrete material form is an absolute necessity of the creative process, also "that matter is not an illusion but a necessary channel through which life differentiates itself."

If you consider matter in its right order as the polar opposite to Spirit, you will not find any antagonism between them. On the contrary, together they constitute one harmonious whole. And when you realize this you feel, in your practice of visualizing, that you are working from cause to effect, from beginning to finish. In reality your mental picture is the specialized working of the originating spirit.

One could talk for hours on purely scientific lines, showing, as Troward says, "that raw material for the formation of the solar systems is universally distributed throughout all space. Yet investigation shows that while the Heavens are studded with millions of suns, there are spaces that show no signs of cosmic activity. This being true, there must be something which started cosmic activity in certain places, while passing over others in which the raw material was equally available. At first thought one might attribute the development of cosmic energy to the etheric particles themselves. Upon investigation, however, we find this to be mathematically impossible in a medium which is equally distributed throughout space, for all its particles are in equilibrium, therefore no one particle possesses in itself a greater power of originating motion than the other.

Thus we find that the initial movement, though working in and through the particles of primary substance, is not the particles themselves. It is this something we mean when we speak of Spirit. The same power that brought universal substance into existence will bring your individual thought or mental picture into physical form. There is no difference of kind in the power. The only difference is a difference of scale. The power and the substance themselves are the same. Only in working out your mental picture it has transferred its creative energy from the universal to the scale of the particular, and is working in the same unfailing manner from its specific center, your mind.

Chapter 4

OPERATION OF YOUR MENTAL PICTURE

The operation of a large telephone system may be used as a simile. The main or head central subdivides itself into many branch centrals, every branch being in direct connection with its source and each individual branch recognizing the source of its existence, reports all things to its central head. Therefore, when assistance of any nature is required, new supplies, difficult repairs to be done or what not, the branch in need goes at once to its central head. It would not think of referring its difficulties (or its successes) to the main central of a telegraph system (though they belong to the same organization). These different branch centrals know that the only remedy for any difficulty must come from the central out of which they were projected.

If we, as individual branches of the Universal Mind, would refer our difficulties in the same confident manner to the source from which we were projected, and use the remedies that it has provided, we would realize what Jesus meant when he said, "Ask and ye shall receive." Our every equipment would be met. Surely the Father must supply the child. The trunk of the tree cannot fail to provide for its branches.

Everything animate or inanimate is called into existence or outstandingness by a power which itself does not stand out. The power that creates the mental picture, the originating spirit substance of your pictured desire does not stand out. It projects the substance of itself that is a solidified counterpart of itself, while it remains invisible to the physical eye. Only those will ever appreciate the value of visualizing who are able to realize Paul's meaning when he said "The worlds were formed by the word of God. Things which are seen are not made of things which do appear."

There is nothing unusual or mysterious in the idea of your pictured desire coming into material evidence. It is the working of a universal natural Law. The world was projected by the self-contemplation of the Universal Mind, and this same action is taking place in its individualized branch which is the Mind of Man. Everything in the whole world has its beginning in mind and comes into existence in exactly the same manner from the hat on your head to the boots on your feet. All are projected thoughts, solidified.

Your personal advance in evolution depends upon your right use of the power of visualizing, and your use of it depends on whether you recognize that you, yourself, are a particular center through and in which the originating spirit is finding ever new expression for potentialities already existing within itself. This is evolution; this continual unfolding of existing though outwardly invisible things.

Your mental picture is the force of attraction that evolves and combines the originating substance into specific shape. Your picture is the combining and evolving powerhouse, so to speak, through which the originating Creative Spirit expressed itself. Its creative action is limitless, without beginning and without end, and always progressive and orderly. "It proceeds stage by stage, each stage being a necessary preparation for the one to follow."

Now let us see if we can get an idea of the different stages by which the things in the world have come to be. Troward says, "If we can get at the working principle which is producing these results, we can very quickly and easily give it personal application. First, we find that the thought of originating life or Spirit about itself is its simple awareness of its own being and this produced a primary ether, a universal substance out of which everything in the world must grow.

Troward also tells us that "though this awareness of being is a necessary foundation for any further possibilities, it is not much to talk about." It is the same with individualized spirit, which is yourself. Before you would entertain the idea of making a mental picture of your desire as being at all practical, you must have some idea of your being, of your "I am," and just as soon as you are conscious of your "I-am-ness" you begin to wish to enjoy the freedom which this consciousness suggests. You want to do more and be more, and as you fulfill this desire within yourself, localized spirit begins conscious activities in you.

The thing you are most concerned with is the specific action of the creative spirit of life, universal mind specialized. The localized God-germ in you is your personality, your individuality, and since the joy of absolute freedom is the inherent nature of this God-germ, it is natural that it should endeavor to enjoy itself through its specific center. And as you grow in the comprehension that your being, your individuality, is God particularizing Himself, you naturally develop Divine tendencies.

You want to enjoy life and liberty. You want freedom in your affairs as well as in your consciousness, and it is natural that you should. Always with this progressive wish there is a faint thought-picture. As your wish and your recognition grow into an intense desire, this desire becomes a clear mental picture. For example, a young lady studying music wishes she had a piano in order to practice at home. She wants the piano so much that she can mentally see it in one of the rooms. She holds the picture of the piano and indulges in the mental reflection of the pleasure and advantage it will be to have the piano in the corner of the living room. One day she finds it there just as she had pictured it.

As you grow in understanding as to who you are, where you came from, and what the purpose of your being is, how you are to fulfill the purpose for which you are intended, you will more and more afford a center through which the creative spirit of life can enjoy itself. And you will realize that there can be but one creative process filling all space, which is the same in its potentiality whether universal or individual. Furthermore, all that there is, whether on the plane of the visible or invisible, had its origin in the localized action of thought or a mental picture, and this includes yourself, because you are universal spirit localized, and the same creative action is taking place through you.

Now you are no doubt asking yourself why there is so much sickness and misery in the world. If the same power and intelligence which brought the world into existence is in operation in the mind of man, why does it not manifest itself as strength, joy, health and plenty? If one can have one's desires fulfilled by simply making a mental picture of that desire, holding on to it with the will, and doing without anxiety, on the outward plane, whatever seems necessary to bring the desire into fulfillment, then there seems no reason for the existence of sickness and poverty. Surely no one desires either.

The first reason is that few persons will take the trouble to inquire into the working principle of the laws of life. If they did they would soon convince themselves that there is no necessity for the sickness and poverty that we see about us. They would realize that visualizing is a principle and not a fallacy.

There are a few who have found it worthwhile to study this simple, though absolutely unfailing law that will deliver them from bondage. However, the race as a whole is not willing to give the time required for this study. It is either too simple, or too difficult. They may make a picture of their desire with some little understanding of visualizing for a day or two, but more frequently it is for an hour or so.

But if you will insist upon mentally seeing yourself surrounded by things and conditions as you wish them to be, you will understand that the creative energy sends its plastic substance in the direction indicated by the tendency of your thoughts. Herein lies the advantage of holding your thought in the form of a mental picture.

The more enthusiasm and faith you are able to put into your picture, the more quickly it will come into visible form, and your enthusiasm is increased by keeping your desire secret. The moment you speak it to any living soul, that moment your power is weakened. Your power, your magnet of attraction is not so strong, and consequently cannot reach so far. The more perfectly a secret between your mind and outer self is guarded, the more vitality you give your power of attraction. One tells one's troubles to weaken them, to get them off one's mind, and when a thought is given out, its power is dissipated. Talk it over with yourself, and even write it down and at once destroy the paper.

However, this does not mean that you should strenuously endeavor to compel the power to work out your picture on the special lines that you think it should. That method would soon exhaust you and hinder the fulfillment of your purpose. A wealthy relative need not necessarily die or someone lose a fortune on the street to materialize the $10,000 that you are mentally picturing.

One of the doormen in the building in which I live heard much of the mental picturing of desires from visitors passing out of my rooms. The average desire was for $500. He considered that five dollars was more in his line and began to visualize it, without the slightest idea of where or how he was to get it. My parrot flew out of the window, and I telephoned to the men in the courtyard to get it for me. One caught it and it bit him on the finger. The doorman, who had gloves on, and did not fear a similar hurt, took hold of it and brought it up to me. I gave him five one-dollar bills for the service. This sudden reward surprised him. He enthusiastically told me that he had been visualizing for just $5, merely from hearing that others visualized. He was delighted at the unexpected realization of his mental picture.

All you have to do is to make such a mental picture of your heart's desire, hold it cheerfully in place with your will, always conscious that the same Infinite Power which brought the universe into existence brought you into form for the purpose of enjoying itself in and through you. And since it is all life, love, light, power, peace, beauty and joy, and is the only creative power there is, the form it takes in and through you depends upon the direction given it by your thought indicator. In you it is undifferentiated, waiting to take any direction given it as it passes through the instrument that it has made for the purpose of self-distribution.

It is this power which enables you to transfer your thoughts from one form to another. The power to change your mind is the individualized universal power taking the initiative, giving direction to the fluent substance contained in every thought. It is the simplest thing in the world to give this highly sensitive plastic substance any form you will through visualizing. Anyone can do it with a small expenditure of effort.

Once you really believe that your mind is a center through which the plastic substance of all there is in your world, takes involuntary form, the only reason why your picture does not always materialize is because you have introduced something antagonistic to the fundamental principle. Very often this destructive element is caused by the frequency with which you change your pictures. After many such changes you decide that your original desire is what you want after all. Upon this conclusion you begin to wonder why, "being your first picture," it hasn't materialized. The plastic substance with which you are mentally dealing is more sensitive than the most sensitive photographer's film. If, in taking a picture, you suddenly remembered you had already taken a picture on that same plate, you would not expect a perfect result of either picture.

On the other hand, you may have taken two pictures on the same plate unconsciously. When the plate has been developed, and the picture comes into physical view, you do not condemn the principle of photography, nor are you puzzled to understand why your picture has turned out so unsatisfactorily. You do not feel that it is impossible for you to obtain a good, clear picture of the subject in question. You know that you can do so, by simply starting at the beginning, putting in a new plate, and determining to be more careful while taking your picture next time. These lines followed out, you are sure of a satisfactory result. If you will proceed in the same manner with your mental picture, doing your part in a correspondingly confident frame of mind, the result will be just as perfect.

The laws of visualizing are as infallible as the laws governing photography. In fact, photography is the outcome of visualizing. Again, your results in visualizing and your desires may be imperfect or delayed through the misuse of this power, owing to the thought that the fulfillment of your desire is contingent upon certain persons or conditions. The originating principle is not in any way dependent upon any person, place or thing. It has no past and knows no future.

The law is that the originating creative principle of life is "the universal here and everlasting now." It creates its own vehicles through which to operate. Therefore, past experience has no bearing upon your present picture. So do not try to obtain your desire through a channel that may not be natural for it, even though it may seem reasonable to you. Your feeling should be that the thing, or the consciousness which you so much desire, is normal and natural, a part of yourself, a form for your evolution. If you can do this, there is no power to prevent your enjoying the fulfillment of the picture you have in hand, or any other.

Chapter 5

EXPRESSIONS FROM BEGINNERS

Hundreds of persons have realized that "visualizing is an Aladdin's lamp to him with a mighty will." General Foch says that his feelings were so outraged during the Franco Prussian war in 1870 that he visualized himself leading a French army against the Germans to victory. He said he made his picture, smoked his pipe and waited. This is one result of visualizing we are all familiar with.

A famous actress wrote a long article in one of the leading Sunday papers last winter, describing how she rid herself of excessive body fat and weight by seeing her figure constantly as she wished to be.

A very interesting letter came to me from a doctor's wife while I was lecturing in New York. She began with the hope that I would never discontinue my lectures on visualization making humanity realize the wonderful fact that they possess the method of liberation within themselves. Relating her own experience, she said that she had been born on the East Side of New York in the poorest quarter. From earliest girlhood she had cherished a dream of marrying a physician some day. This dream gradually formed a stationary mental picture. The first position she obtained was in the capacity of a nursemaid in a physician's family.

Leaving this place she entered the family of another doctor. The wife of her employer died, and in time the doctor married her, the result of her long-pictured yearning. After that both she and her husband conceived the idea of owning a fruit farm in the South. They formed a mental picture of the idea and put their faith in its eventual fulfillment. The letter she sent me came from their fruit farm in the South. It was while at the farm that the doctor's wife wrote me. Her second mental picture had seen the light of materialization.

Many letters of a similar nature come to me every day. The following is a case that was printed in the New York Herald last May:

"Atlantic City, May 5. - She was an old woman, and when she was arraigned before Judge Clarence Goldenberg in the police court today she was so weak and tired she could hardly stand. The judge asked the court attendant what she was charged with. "Stealing a bottle of milk, Your Honor," repeated the officer. "She took it from the doorstep of a downtown cottage before daybreak this morning." "Why did you do that?" Judge Goldenberg asked her. "I was hungry," the old woman said. "I didn't have a cent in the world and no way to get anything to eat except to steal it. I didn't think anybody would mind if I took a bottle of milk." "What's your name?" asked the judge. "Weinberg," said the old woman, "Elizabeth Weinberg." Judge Goldenberg asked her a few questions about herself. Then he said:

"Well, you're not very wealthy now, but you're no longer poor. I've been searching for you for months. I've got $500 belonging to you from the estate of a relative. I am the executor of the estate."

Judge Goldenberg paid the woman's fine out of his own pocket, and then escorted her into his office, where he turned her legacy over to her and sent a policeman out to find her a lodging place.

I learned later that this little woman had been desiring and mentally picturing $500, while all the time ignorant of how it could possibly come to her. But she kept her vision and strengthened it with her faith.

In a recent issue of Good Housekeeping there was an article by Addington Bruce entitled "Stiffening Your Mental Backbone." It is very instructive, and would benefit anyone to read it. He says, in part: "Form the habit of devoting a few moments every day to thinking about your work in a large, broad imaginative way, as a vital necessity to yourself and a useful service to society."

Huntington, the great railway magnate, before he started building his road from coast to coast, said that he took hundreds of trips all along the line before there was a rail laid. It is said that he would sit for hours with a map of the United States before him and mentally travel from coast to coast just as we do now over his fulfilled mental picture. It would be possible to call your attention to hundreds of similar cases.

The best method of picturing to yourself that which you may desire is both simple and enjoyable, if you once understand the principle back of it well enough to believe it. First and above everything else, be sure of what it is you really want. Then specialize your desire along these lines.

Chapter 6

SUGGESTIONS FOR MAKING YOUR MENTAL PICTURE

Perhaps you want to feel that you've lived to some purpose. You want to be content and happy, and you feel that with good health and with successful business you could enjoy this state of mind. After you have decided once and for all that this is what you want, you proceed to picture yourself healthy, and your business just as great a success as you can naturally conceive it growing into.

The best time for making your definite picture is just before breakfast and before retiring at night. As it is necessary to give yourself plenty of time, it may be necessary to rise earlier than is your usual habit. Go into a room where you will not be disturbed, meditate for a few moments upon the practical working of the law of visualizing, and ask yourself, "How did the things about me first come into existence? How may I find it helpful to get more quickly in touch with the invisible supply?"

Someone felt that comfort would be better expressed and experienced by sitting on a chair than on the floor. The very beginning of the meditation, the chair, was the desire to be at ease. With this came the picture of some sort of a chair. The same principle applies to the hat and the clothes that you wear. Go carefully into this thought of the principle back of the thing. Establish it as a personal experience; make it a fact to your consciousness.

If you are thorough in this, you will find yourself in the deep consciousness beneath the surface of your own thought-power. Then open a window, take about ten deep breaths, and during the time draw a large imaginary circle of light around you. As you inhale (keeping yourself in the center of this circle of light) see great rays of light coming from the circle and entering your body at all points, centralizing itself at your solar plexus.

Hold the breath a few moments at this central light of your body (the solar plexus) then slowly exhale. As you do this mentally, see imaginary rays, or sprays, of light going up through the body and down and out through the feet. Mentally spray your entire body with this imaginary light. When you have finished the breathing exercise, sit in a comfortable upright chair and mentally know there is but one life, one substance, and this life substance of the universe is finding pleasure in self-recognition in you. Repeat some affirmation of this kind, until you feel the truth and reality of the words that you are affirming. Then begin your picture.

Whether your desire is for a state of consciousness or a possession, large or small, begin at the beginning. If you want a house, begin by seeing yourself in the kind of house you desire. Go all through it, taking careful note of the rooms, where the windows are situated, and such other details as help you to feel the reality of your concept.

You might change some of the furniture and look into some of the mirrors just to see how healthy, wealthy and happy you look. Go over your picture again and again until you feel the reality of it, then write it all down just as you have seen it, with the feeling that, "The best there is, is mine. There is no limit to me, because my mind is a center of divine operation" and your picture is as certain to come true, in your physical world, as the sun is to shine.

Chapter 7

THINGS TO REMEMBER

In Using Your Thought Power for the Production of New Conditions,

1. Be sure to know what conditions you wish to produce. Then weigh carefully to what further results the accomplishment of your desire will lead.

2. By letting your thought dwell upon a mental picture, you are concentrating the creative spirit to this center, where all its forces are equally balanced.

3. Visualizing brings your objective mind into a state of equilibrium which enables you to consciously direct the flow of spirit to a definitely recognized purpose and to carefully guide your thought from including a flow in the opposite direction.

4. You must always bear in mind that you are dealing with a wonderful potential energy - which is not yet differentiated into any particular mould, and that by the action of your mind you can differentiate it into any specific mould that you will. Your picture assists you to keep your mind fixed on the fact that the inflow of this creative energy is taking place. Also by your mental picture you are determining the direction you wish the sensitive creative power to take, and by doing this the externalization of your picture is a certainty.

5. Remember when you are visualizing properly that there is no strenuous effort on your thoughts to hold your thought -forms in place. Strenuous effort defeats your purpose, and suggests the consciousness of an adverse force to be fought against, and this creates conditions adverse to your picture.

6. By holding your picture in a cheerful frame of mind, you shut out all thoughts that would disperse the spiritual nucleus of your picture. Because the law is creative in its action, your pictured desire is certain of accomplishment.

7. The seventh and great thing to remember in visualizing is that you are making a mental picture for the purpose of determining the quality you are giving to the previously undifferentiated substance and energy rather than to arrange the specific circumstances for its manifestation. That is the work of creative power itself. It will build its own forms of expression quite naturally, if you will allow it, and save you a great deal of needless anxiety. What you really want is expansion in a certain direction, whether of health, wealth, or what not, and so long as you get it (as you surely will, if you confidently hold to your picture) what does it matter whether it reaches you by some channel which you thought you could count upon, or through some other of whose existence you had no idea. You are concentrating energy of a particular kind for a particular purpose. Bear this in mind and let specific details take care of themselves, and never mention your intention to anyone.

Remember always, that Nature from her clearly visible surface to her most arcane depths is one vast storehouse of light and good entirely devoted to your individual use. Your conscious Oneness with the great Whole is the secret of success and when once you have fathomed this you can enjoy your possession of the whole or a part of it at will, because by your recognition you have made it, and can increasingly make it yours.

Never forget that every physical thing, whether for you or against you, was a sustained thought before it was a thing.

Thought as thought is neither good nor bad, it is creative action and always takes physical form.

Therefore, the thoughts you dwell upon become the things you possess or do not possess.

Chapter 8

WHY I TOOK UP THE STUDY OF MENTAL SCIENCE

I have frequently been questioned about my reasons for taking up the study of Mental Science, and as to the results of my search, not only in knowledge of principles, but also in the application of that knowledge to the development of my own life and experience.

Such inquiries are justifiable, because one who essays the role of a messenger and teacher of psychological truths can only be effective and convincing as he or she has tested them in the laboratory of mental experience. This is particularly true in my case, as the only personal pupil of Thomas Troward, the greatest Master of Mental Science of the present day, whose teaching is based upon the relation borne by the Individual Mind toward the Universal Creative Mind which is the Giver of Life, and the manner in which that relation may be invoked to secure expansion and fuller expression in the individual life.

The initial impulse toward the study of Mental Science was an overwhelming sense of loneliness. In every life there must come some such experiences of spiritual isolations as, at that period, pervaded my life. Notwithstanding the fact that each day found me in the midst of friends, surrounded by mirth and gayety, there was a persistent feeling that I was alone in the world. I had been a widow for about three years, wandering from country to country, seeking for peace of mind.

The circumstances and surroundings of my life were such that my friends looked upon me as an unusually fortunate young woman. Although they recognized that I had sustained a great loss when my husband died, they knew that he had left me well provided for, free to go anywhere at pleasure, and having many friends. Yet, if my friends could have penetrated my inmost emotions, they would have found a deep sense of emptiness and isolation. This feeling inspired a spirit of unrest that drove me on and on in fruitless search upon the outside for that which I later learned could only be obtained from within.

I studied Christian Science, but it gave me no solace, though fully realizing the great work the Scientists were doing, and even having the pleasure and privilege of meeting Mrs. Eddy personally. But it was impossible for me to accept the fundamental teachings of Christian Science and make practical application of it.

When about to abandon the search for contentment and resign myself to resume a life of apparent amusement, a friend invited me to visit the great Seer and Teacher, Abdul Baha. After my interview with this most wonderful of men, my search for contentment began to take a change. He had told me that I would travel the world over seeking the truth, and when I had found it would speak it out. The fulfillment of the statement of this Great Seer then seemed to be impossible. But it carried a measure of encouragement, and at least indicated that my former seeking had been in the wrong direction. I began in a feeble and groping way to find contentment within myself, for had he not intimated that I should find the truth. That was the big thing, and about the only thing I remember of our interview.

A few days later, upon visiting the office of a New Thought practitioner, my attention was attracted to a book on his table entitled "The Edinburgh Lectures on Mental Science," by Thomas Troward. It interested me to see that Troward was a retired Divisional judge from the Punjab, India. I purchased the book, thinking I would read it through that evening. Many have endeavored to do the same thing, only to find, as I did, that the book must be studied in order to be understood, and hundreds have decided, just as I did, to give it their undivided attention.

After finding this treasure book I went to the country for a few days, and while there studied the volume as thoroughly as I could. It seemed extremely difficult, and I decided to purchase another book of Troward's, in the hope that its study might not require so much of an effort. Upon inquiry I was told that a subsequent volume, "The Dore Lectures," was much the simpler and better of the two books. When I procured it, I found that it must also be studied. It took me weeks and months to get even a vague conception of the meaning of the first chapter of Dore, which is entitled "Entering Into the Spirit of It." I mean by this that it took me months to enter into the spirit of what I was reading.

But in the meantime a paragraph from page 26 arrested my attention, as seeming the greatest thing I had ever read. I memorized it and endeavored with all my soul to enter into the spirit of Troward's words. The paragraph reads: "My mind is a center of Divine operation. The Divine operation is always for expansion and fuller expression, and this means the production of something beyond what has gone before, something entirely new, not included in the past experience, though proceeding out of it by an orderly sequence of growth. Therefore, since the Divine cannot change its inherent nature, it must operate in the same manner with me; consequently, in my own special world, of which I am the center, it will move forward to produce new conditions, always in advance of any that have gone before."

It took an effort on my part to memorize this paragraph, but in the endeavor toward this end the words seemed to carry with them a certain stimulus. Each repetition of the paragraph made it easier for me to enter into the spirit of it. The words expressed exactly what I had been seeking for. My one desire was for peace of mind. I found it comforting to believe that the Divine operation in me could expand to fuller expression and produce more and more contentment -in fact, a peace of mind and a degree of contentment greater than I had ever known. The paragraph further inspired me with deep interest to feel that the life-spark in me could bring into my life something entirely new. I did not wish to obliterate my past experience, but that was exactly what Troward said it would not do. The Divine operation would not exclude my past experience, but proceeding out of them would bring some new thing that would transcend anything that I had ever experienced before.

Meditation on these statements brought with it a certain joyous feeling. What a wonderful thing it would be if I could accept and sincerely believe, beyond all doubt, that this one statement of Troward's was true. Surely the Divine could not change its inherent nature, and since Divine life is operating in me, I must be Divinely inhabited, and the Divine in me must operate just as it operates upon the Universal plane. This meant that my whole world of circumstances, friends and conditions would ultimately become a world of contentment and enjoyment of which "I am the center." This would all happen just as soon as I was able to control my mind and thereby provide concrete center around which the Divine energies could play.

Surely it was worth trying for. If Troward had found this truth, why not I? The idea held me to my task. Later I determined to study with the man who had realized and given to the world so great a statement. It had lifted me from my state of despondency. The immediate difficulty was the need for increased finances.

Chapter 9

HOW I ATTRACTED TO MYSELF TWENTY THOUSAND DOLLARS

In the laboratory of experience in which my newly revealed relation to Divine operation was to be tested, the first problem was a financial one. My income was a stipulated one, quite enough for my everyday needs. But it did not seem sufficient to enable me to go comfortably to England where Troward lived, and remain for an indefinite period to study with so great a teacher as he must be. So before inquiring whether Troward took pupils or whether I would be eligible in case he did, I began to use the paragraph I had memorized. Daily, in fact, almost hourly, the words were in my mind: "My mind is a center of Divine operation, and Divine operation means expansion into something better than has gone before."

From the Edinburgh Lectures I had read something about the Law of Attraction, and from the Chapter of "Causes and Conditions" I had gleaned a vague idea of visualizing. So every night, before going to sleep, I made a mental picture of the desired $20,000. Twenty $1,000 bills were counted over each night in my bedroom, and then, with the idea of more emphatically impressing my mind with the fact that this twenty thousand dollars was for the purpose of going to England and studying with Troward, I wrote out my picture, saw myself buying my steamer ticket, walking up and down the ship's deck from New York to London, and, finally, saw myself accepted as Troward's pupil.

This process was repeated every morning and every evening, always impressing more and more fully upon my mind Troward's memorized statement: "My mind is a center of Divine operations." I endeavored to keep this statement in the back part of my consciousness all the time with no thought in mind as how the money might be obtained. Probably the reason why there was no thought of the avenues through which the money might reach me was because I could not possibly imagine where the $20,000 would come from. So I simply held my thought steady and let the power of attraction find its own ways and means.

One day while walking on the street, taking deep breathing exercises, the thought came: "My mind is surely a center of Divine operation. If God fills all space, then God must be in my mind also; if I want this money to study with Troward that I may know the truth of Life, then both the money and the truth must be mine, though I am unable to feel or see the physical manifestations of either; still," I declared, "it must be mine."

While these reflections were going on in my mind, there seemed to come up from within me the thought: "I am all the substance there is." Then, from another channel in my brain the answer seemed to come, "Of course, that's it; everything must have its beginning in mind. The "I" the Idea, must be the only one and primary substance there is, and this means money as well as everything else." My mind accepted this idea, and immediately all the tension of mind and body was relaxed.

There was a feeling of absolute certainty of being in touch with all the power Life has to give. All thought of money, teacher, or even my own personality, vanished in the great wave of joy which swept over my entire being. I walked on and on with this feeling of joy steadily increasing and expanding until everything about me seemed aglow with resplendent light. Every person I passed was illuminated as I was. All consciousness of personality had disappeared, and in its place there came that great and almost overwhelming sense of joy and contentment.

That night when I made my picture of the twenty thousand dollars it was with an entirely changed aspect. On previous occasions, when making my mental picture, I had felt that I was waking up something within myself. This time there was no sensation of effort. I simply counted over the twenty thousand dollars. Then, in a most unexpected manner, from a source of which I had no consciousness at the time, there seemed to open a possible avenue through which the money might reach me.

At first it took great effort not to be excited. It all seemed so wonderful, so glorious to be in touch with supply. But had not Troward cautioned his readers to keep all excitement out of their minds in the first flush of realization of union with Infinite supply, and to treat this fact as a perfectly natural result that had been reached through our demand? This was even more difficult for me than it was to hold the thought that "all the substance there is, I am; I (idea) am the beginning of all form, visible or invisible."

Just as soon as there appeared a circumstance which indicated the direction through which the twenty thousand dollars might come, I not only made a supreme effort to regard the indicated direction calmly as the first sprout of the seed I had sown in the absolute, but left no stone unturned to follow up that direction by fulfilling my part. By so doing one circumstance seemed naturally to lead to another, until, step-by-step, my desired twenty thousand dollars was secured. To keep my mind poised and free from excitement was my greatest effort.

This first concrete fruition of my study of Mental Science as expounded by Troward's book had come by a careful following of the methods he had outlined. In this connection, therefore, I can offer to the reader no better gift than to quote Troward's book, "The Edinburgh Lectures," from which may be derived a complete idea of the line of action I was endeavoring to follow. In the chapter on Causes and Conditions he says: "To get good results we must properly understand our relation to the great impersonal power we are using. It is intelligent, and we are intelligent, and the two intelligences must co-operate.

We must not fly in the face of the Law expecting it to do for us what it can only do through us; and we must therefore use our intelligence with the knowledge that it is acting as the instrument of a greater intelligence; and because we have this knowledge we may and should cease from all anxiety as to the final result.

In actual practice we must first form the ideal conception of our object with the definite intention of impressing it upon the universal mind -it is this thought that takes such thought out of the region of mere casual fancies-and then affirm that our knowledge of the Law is sufficient reason for a calm expectation of a corresponding result, and that therefore all necessary conditions will come to us in due order. We can then turn to the affairs of our daily life with the calm assurance that the initial conditions are either there already or will soon come into view. If we do not at once see them, let us rest content with the knowledge that the spiritual prototype is already in existence and wait till some circumstance pointing in the desired direction begins to show itself.

It may be a very small circumstance, but it is the direction and not the magnitude that is to be taken into consideration. As soon as we see it we should regard it as the first sprouting of the seed sown in the Absolute, and do calmly, and without excitement, whatever the circumstances seem to require, and then later on we shall see that this doing will in turn lead to a further circumstance in the same direction, until we find ourselves conducted, step by step, to the accomplishment of our object.

In this way the understanding of the great principle of the Law of Supply will, by repeated experiences, deliver us more and more completely out of the region of anxious thought and toilsome labor and bring us into a new world where the useful employment of all our powers, whether mental or physical, will only be an unfolding of our individuality upon the lines of its own nature, and therefore a perpetual source of health and happiness; a sufficient inducement, surely, to the careful study of the laws governing the relation between the individual and the Universal Mind."

To my mind, then as now, this quotation outlines the core and center of the method and manner of approach necessary for coming in touch with Infinite supply. At least it, together with the previously quoted statement, "My mind is a center of Divine operation," etc., constituted the only apparent means of attracting to myself the twenty thousand dollars. My constant endeavor to get into the spirit of these statements, and to attract to myself this needed sum, was about six weeks, at the end of which time I had in my bank the required twenty thousand dollars. This could be made into a long story, giving all the details, but the facts, as already narrated, will give you a definite idea of the magnetic condition of my mind while the twenty thousand dollars was finding its way to me.

HOW I BECAME THE ONLY PERSONAL PUPIL OF THE GREATEST MENTAL SCIENTIST OF THE PRESENT DAY

As soon as the idea of studying with Troward came to me, I asked a friend to write to him for me, feeling that perhaps my friend could put my desire in better or more persuasive terms than I could employ. To all the letters written by this friend I received not one reply. This was so discouraging that I would have completely abandoned the idea of becoming Troward's pupil except for the experience I had that day on the street when my whole world was illuminated, and I remembered the promise "All things whatsoever thou wilt, believe thou hast received, and thou shalt receive."

With this experience in my mind, my passage to England was arranged, notwithstanding the fact that apparently my letters were ignored. We wrote again, however, and finally received a reply, very courteous though very positive. Troward did not take pupils; he had no time to devote to a pupil. Notwithstanding this definite decision, I declined to be discouraged because of the memory of my experience upon the day when the light and the thought came to me, "I am all the Substance there is." I seemed to be able to live that experience over at will, and with it there always came a flood of courage and renewed energy. We journeyed on to London, and from there telegraphed Troward, asking for an interview. The telegram was promptly answered by Troward setting a date when he could see us.

At this time Troward was living in Ruan Manor, a little-out-of-the-way place in the southern part of England, about twenty miles from a railway station. We could not find it on the map, and with great difficulty Cook's Touring Agency in London, located the place for us. There was very little speculation in my mind as to what Troward would say to me in this interview. There always remained the feeling that the truth was mine; also that it would grow and expand in my consciousness until peace and contentment were outward as well as inward manifestations of my individual life.

We arrived at Troward's house in a terrific rainstorm, and were cordially received by Troward himself, whom I found, much to my surprise, to be more the type of a Frenchman than an Englishman (I afterward learned that he was a descendant of the Huguenot race), a man of medium stature, with rather a large head, big nose, and eyes that fairly danced with merriment. After we had been introduced to the other members of the family and given a hot cup of tea, we were invited into the living room where Troward talked very freely of everything except my proposed studies. It seemed quite impossible to bring him to that subject.

Just before we were leaving, however, I asked quite boldly: "Will you not reconsider your decision to take a personal pupil? I wish so much to study with you," to which he replied with a very indifferent manner that he did not feel he could give the time it would require for personal instruction, but that he would be glad to give me the names of two or three books which he felt would not only be interesting but instructive to me. He said he felt much flattered and pleased that I had come all the way from America to study with him, and as we walked out through the lane from his house to our automobile his manner became less indifferent, a feeling of sympathy seemed to touch his heart, and he turned to me with the remark: "You might write to me, if so inclined, after you get to Paris, and perhaps, if I have time in the autumn, we could arrange something, though it does not seem possible now."

I lost no time in following up his very kind invitation to write. My letters were all promptly and courteously answered, but there was never a word of encouragement as to my proposed studies. Finally, about two months later, there came a letter with the question in it: "What do you suppose is the meaning of this verse in the 21st Chapter of Revelation?"

"16. And the city lieth foursquare and the length is as large as the breadth; and he measured the city with the reed, twelve thousand furlongs. The length and the breadth and the height of it are equal."

Instinctively I knew that my chance to study with Troward hung upon my giving the correct answer to that question. The definition of the verse seemed utterly beyond my reach. Naturally, answers came to my mind, but I knew intuitively that none was correct. I began bombarding my scholarly friends and acquaintances with the same question. Lawyers, doctors, priests, nuns and clergymen, all over the world, received letters from me with this question in them. Later answers began to return to me, but intuition told me that none was correct. All the while I was endeavoring to find the answer for myself, but none seemed to come. I memorized the verse in order that I might meditate upon it.

I began a search of Paris for the books Troward had recommended to me, and after two or three days' search we crossed the River Seine to the Ile de Cite to go into some of the old bookstores there. They were out of print, and these were the best places to find them in. Finally we came upon a little shop that had the books there. These were the last copies the man had, consequently the price was high. While remonstrating with the clerk, my eye rested upon the work of an astrologer, which I laughingly picked up and asked: "Do you think Prof. would read my horoscope?" The clerk looked aghast at the suggestion, and responded, "Why, no, Madame, this is one of France's greatest astrologers. He does not read horoscopes."

In spite of this answer, there was a persistent impulse within me to go to the man. The friend who had accompanied me in my search for the books remonstrated with me, and tried in every way to dissuade me from going to the famous astrologer, but I insisted, and she went with me. When we came to his office I found it somewhat embarrassing to ask him to read my horoscope. Nevertheless, there was nothing to do but put the question. Reluctantly, the Professor invited us into his paper-strewn study, and reluctantly, and also impatiently, asked us to be seated. Very courteously and coldly he told me that he did not read horoscopes. His whole manner said, more clearly than words could, that he wished we would take our departure.

My friend stood up. I was at a great loss what to do next, because I felt that I was not quite ready to go. Intuition seemed to tell me there was something for me to gain there. Just what it was I was unable to define, so I paused a moment, much to my friend's displeasure, when one of the Professor's enormous Persian cats jumped into my lap. "Get down, Jack!" the Professor shouted. "What does it mean?" he seemed to ask himself. Then with a greater interest than he had hitherto shown in me, the Professor said with a smile: "Have never known that cat to go to a stranger before, Madame; my cat pleads for you." I, also, now feel an interest in your horoscope, and if you will give me the data it will give me pleasure to write it out for you." There was a great feeling of happiness in me when he made this statement. He concluded by saying: "I do not feel that you really care for your horoscope." The truth of this statement shocked me, because I did not care about a horoscope, and could not give any reason why I was letting him do it. "However," he said, "May I call for your data next Sunday afternoon?"

On Sunday afternoon at the appointed time, the Professor arrived, and I was handing him the slip of paper with all the data of my birth, etc., when the idea came to me to ask the Professor for the answer to the question about the 16th verse of the 21st Chapter of Revelation. The thought was instantly carried into effect, and I found myself asking this man what he thought this verse meant. Without pausing to think it over he immediately replied "it means: The city signifies the truth, and the truth is non-invertible; every side from which you approach it is exactly the same." Intuitively and undoubtingly I recognized this answer as the true one, and my joy knew no bounds, because I felt sure that with this correct answer in my possession, Troward would accept me as his pupil in the fall.

As the great astrologer was leaving, I explained to him all about my desire to study with Troward, how I had come from New York City for that express purpose, seemingly to no avail, until the answer to this test question had been given to me by him. He was greatly interested

35

and asked many questions about Troward, and when asked if he would please send me his bill, he smilingly replied, "Let me know if the great Troward accepts you as his pupil," and bade me good afternoon. I hastened to my room to send a telegram to Troward giving my answer to the question about the 16th verse of the 21st Chapter of Revelation.

There was an immediate response from Troward that said: "Your answer is correct. Am beginning a course of lectures on The Great Pyramid In London. If you wish to attend them, will be pleased to have you, and afterward, if you still wish to study with me, I think it can be arranged." On receipt of this reply preparations were at once made to leave Paris for London.

I attended all the lectures, receiving much instruction from them, after which arrangements were made for my studying with Troward. Two days before leaving for Cornwall I received the following letter from Troward clearly indicating the line of study he gave me:

31 Stanwick Road,
  W. Kensington, England,
  November 8, 1912.

Dear Mrs. Behrend,

I think I had better write you a few lines with regard to your proposed studies with me, as I should be sorry for you to be under any misapprehension and so to suffer any disappointment.

I have studied the subject now for several years, and have a general acquaintance with the leading features of most of the systems which, unfortunately, occupy attention in many circles at the present time, such as Theosophy, The Tarot, The Kabala, and the like, and I have no hesitation in saying that, to the best of my judgment, all sorts and descriptions of so-called occult study are in direct opposition to the real life-giving Truth, and, therefore, you must not expect any teaching on such lines as these.

We hear a great deal these days about Initiation; but, believe me, the more you try to become a so-called "Initiate" the further you will put yourself from living life. I speak after many years of careful study and consideration when I say that the Bible and its Revelation of Christ is the one thing really worth studying, and th at is a subject large enough in all conscience, embracing, as it does, our outward life and of everyday concerns, and also the inner springs of our life and all that we can in general terms conceive of the life in the unseen after putting off the body at death.

You have expressed a very great degree of confidence in my teaching, and if your confidence is such that you wish, as you say, to put yourself entirely under my guidance, I can only accept it as a very serious responsibility, and should have to ask you to exhibit that confidence by refusing to look into such so-called "Mysteries" as I would forbid you to look into.

I am speaking from experience; but the result will be that much of my teaching will appear to be very simple, perhaps to some extent dogmatic, and you will say you have heard much of it before.

Faith in God, Prayer and Worship, approach to the Father through Christ -all this is in a certain sense familiar to you; and all I can hope to do is perhaps to throw a little more light on these subjects, that they may become to you, not merely traditional words, but present living facts.

I have been thus explicit as I do not want you to have any disappointment, and also I should say that our so-called course of study will be only friendly conversations at such times as we can fit them in, either you coming to our house, or I to yours, as may be most convenient at the time.

Also, I will lend you some books that will be helpful, but they are very few, and in no sense occult.

Now, if all this falls in with your ideas, we shall, I am sure, be very glad to see you at Ruan Manor, and you will find that the residents there, though few, are very friendly and the neighborhood very pretty.

But, on the other hand, if you feel that you want some other source of learning, do not mind saying so, only you will never find any substitute for Christ.

I trust you will not mind my writing you like this, but I do not want you to come all the way down to Cornwall, and then be disappointed.

With kindest regards,

Yours sincerely,

(Signed) T. TROWARD.

This copy of Troward's letter, to my mind, is the greatest thing I can give you.

Chapter 11

HOW TO BRING THE POWER IN YOUR WORD INTO ACTION

In your every word there is the power germ that expands and projects itself in the direction your word indicates, and ultimately develops into physical expression. For example, you wish to establish joy in your consciousness. Just repeat the word "joy" secretly, persistently and emphatically. The joy germ begins to expand and project itself until your whole being is filled with joy. This is not a mere fancy, but a truth. Once you experience this power, you will "daily prove that these facts have not been fabricated to fit a theory, but the theory has been built up by careful observation of facts." Everyone knows that joy comes from within. Another may give you cause for joy, but no one can be joyous for you. Joy is a state of consciousness, and consciousness is purely Troward says, "Mental."

Mental faculties always work under something which stimulates them, and this stimulus may come either from without, through the external senses, or from within by the consciousness of something not perceptible on the physical plane. The recognition of this interior source of stimulus enables you to bring into your consciousness any state you "desire." Once a thing seems normal to you, it is as surely yours, through the law of growth and attraction, as it is yours to know addition after you have the conscious use of figures.

This method of repeating the word makes the word in all of its limitless meaning yours, because words are the embodiment of thoughts, and thought is creative, neither good nor bad, simply creative. This is the reason why Faith builds up and Fear destroys. "Only believe, and all things are possible unto you." It is Faith that gives you dominion over every adverse circumstance or condition. It is your word of faith that sets you free, not faith in any specific thing or act, but simple Faith in your best self in all ways. It is because of this ever-present creative power within the heart of the word that makes your health, your peace of mind and your financial condition a reproduction of your most habitual thought. Try to believe and understand this, and you will find yourself Master of every adverse circumstance or condition, a Prince of Power.

Chapter 12

HOW TO INCREASE YOUR FAITH

But, you ask - How can I speak the word of Faith when I have little or no faith? Every living thing has faith in something or somebody. It is the quality of the creative energy in the positive Faith thought which gives it vitality, not the form it takes. Even intense fear is alive with faith. You fear smallpox because you believe it possible for you to contract it. You fear poverty and loneliness because you believe them possible for you.

It is your habitual tendency of thought that reappears in your mind, your body and your affairs, not the occasional thought upon some specific line or desire. It is the Faith which understands that every creation hadits birth in the womb of thought -words that gives you dominion over all things, your lesser self included, and this feeling of faith is increased and intensified through observing what it does.

This observation is the observation of your state of consciousness when you did, not when you hoped you might, but feared it was too good to be true. How did you feel that time when you simply had to bring yourself into a better frame of mind and did, or you had to have a certain thing and got it? Live these experiences over again and again (mentally) until you really feel in touch with the self that knows and does, and the best there is, is yours.

Chapter 13

THE REWARD OF INCREASED FAITH

Because you have expanded your faith into the faith and laws of the universe that know no failure, your faith in the best of yourself (the principle of life in you) has brought you into conscious realization that you are not a victim of the universe, but a part of it. Consequently, there is that within yourself which is able to make conscious contact with the universal principal of law and power, and enables you to press all the particular laws of nature, whether visible or invisible, into serving your particular demand or desire, and thereby you find yourself Master, not a slave of any situation.

Troward tells us that this Mastering is to be "accomplished by knowledge, and the only knowledge which will afford this purpose in all its measureless immensity is the knowledge of the personal element in universal spirit" and its reciprocity to our own personality. In other words, the words you think, the personality you feel yourself to be, are all reproductions in miniature or specialized God "or universal spirit." All your word-thoughts were God word-forms before they were yours.

The words you use are the instruments, channels, through which the creative energy takes shape. Naturally, this sensitive creative power can only reproduce in accordance with the instrument through which it passes. All disappointments and failures are the result of endeavoring to think one thing and produce another. This is just as impossible as it would be for an electric fan to be used for lighting purposes, or for water to flow through a crooked pipe in a straight line.

The water must take the shape of the pipe through which it flows. Even more truly this sensitive, invisible, fluent substance must reproduce outwardly the shape of the thought-word through which it passes. This is the law of its nature; therefore, it logically follows, "As a man thinketh, so is he." Hence, when your thought or word-form is in correspondence with the Eternal constructive and forward movement of the Universal Law, then your mind is the mirror in which the infinite power and intelligence of the universe sees itself reproduced,and your individual life becomes one of harmony.

Chapter 14

HOW TO MAKE NATURE RESPOND TO YOU

It should be steadily borne in mind that there is an intelligence and power in all nature and all space that is always creative and infinitely sensitive and responsive. The responsiveness of its nature is two-fold: it is creative and amenable to suggestion. Once the human understanding grasps this all-important fact, it realizes the simplicity of the law of life.

All that is necessary is to realize that your mind is a center of Divine operation, and consequently contains that within itself which accepts suggestions, and expect all life to respond to your call, and you will find suggestions which tend to the fulfillment of your desire coming to you, not only from your fellowmen, but also from the flowers, the grass, the trees and the rocks which will enable you to fulfill your heart's desire, if you act upon them in confidence on this physical plane. "Faith without works is dead," but Faith with Works sets you absolutely free.

Chapter 15

FAITH WITH WORKS – WHAT IT HAS ACCOMPLISHED

It is said of Tyson, the great Australian millionaire, that the suggestion to "make the desert land of Australia blossom as the rose" came to him from a modest little Australian violet while he was working as a bushman for something like three shillings a day. He used to find these friendly little violets growing in certain places in the woods, and something in the flower touched something akin to itself in the mind of Tyson, and he would sit on the side of his bunk at night and wonder how flowers and vegetable life could be given an opportunity to express itself in the desert land of Australia.

No doubt he realized that it would take a long time to save enough money to put irrigating ditches in the desert lands, but his thought and feeling were sure it could be accomplished, and if it could be done, he could do it. If there was a power within himself that was able to capture the idea, then there must be a responsive power within the idea itself that could bring itself into a practical physical manifestation. He resolutely put aside all questions as to the specific ways and means which would be employed in bringing his desire into physical manifestation, and simply kept his thought centered upon the idea of making fences and seeing flowers and grass where none existed.

Since the responsiveness of reproductive creative power is not limited to any local condition of mind, his habitual meditation and mental picture set his ideas free to roam in an infinitude, and attract to themselves other ideas of a kindred nature. Therefore, it was not necessary for Tyson to wait and see his ideas and desires fulfilled, until he had saved from his three shillings a day enough money to irrigate the land,for his ideas found other ideas in the financial world which were attuned in sympathy with themselves, and doors of finance were quickly opened.

All charitable institutions are maintained upon the principle of the responsiveness of life. If this were not true, no one would care to give, simply because another needed. The law of demand and supply, cause and effect, can never be broken. Ideas attract to themselves kindred ideas. Sometimes they come from a flower, a book or out of the invisible. You are sitting or walking, intent upon an idea not quite complete as to the ways and means of fulfillment, and behold along comes another idea, from no one can tell where, and finds friendly lodging with your idea, one idea attracting another, and so on until your desires are physical facts.

You may feel the necessity for an improvement in your finances, and wonder how this increase is to be brought about, when there seems suddenly to come from within the idea that everything had its birth in thought, even money, and your thoughts turn their course. You simply hold to the statement or affirmation that the best, and all there is, is yours. Since you are able to capture ideas from the Infinite through the instrument of your intuition, you let your mind rest upon that thought knowing full well that this very thought will respond to itself. Your inhibition of the thought of doubt and feeling of anxiety enables the reassuring ideas to establish themselves and attract to themselves "I can" and "I will" ideas, which gradually grow into physical form of the desire in mind.

In the conscious use of the universal power to reproduce your desires in physical form, three facts should be borne in mind:

First - All space is filled with a creative power. Second - This creative power is amenable to suggestion. Third - It can only work by deductive methods.

As Troward tells us, this last is an exceedingly important point, for it implies that the action of the ever-present creative power is in no way limited by precedent. It works according to the essence of the spirit of the principle. In other words, this universal power takes its creative direction from the word you give it. Once man realizes this great truth, it becomes the most important of all his consideration with what character this sensitive reproductive power is invested. It is the unvarying law of this creative life principle that "As a man thinketh in his heart so is he." If you realize the truth that the only creative power can be to you only what you feel and think it to be, it is willing and able to meet your demands.

Troward says, "If you think your thought is Powerful, then your Thought is Powerful." "As a man thinketh in his heart, so is he" is the law of life, and the creative power can no more change this law than an ordinary mirror can reflect back to you a different image than the object you hold before it. "As you think so are you" does not mean "as you tell people you think" or "as you would wish the world to believe you think." It means your innermost thoughts, that place where no one but you knows. "None can know the Father save the son" and "No one can know the son but the Father."

Only the reproductive creative spirit of life knows what you think until your thoughts become physical facts and manifest themselves in your body, your brain or your affairs. Then everyone with whom you come into contact may know, because the Father, the intelligent creative energy which heareth in secret, hears your most secret thoughts, rewards you openly, reproduces your thoughts in physical form. "As you think you know that is what you become" should be kept in the background of your mind constantly. This is watching and praying without ceasing, and when you are not feeling quite up to par to physically pray.

Chapter 16

SUGGESTIONS AS TO HOW TO PRAY OR ASK, BELIEVING YOU HAVE ALREADY RECEIVED

Scientific Thinking - Positive Thought

Suggestions for Practical Application:

Try, through careful, positive, enthusiastic (though not strenuous) thought, to realize that the indescribable,invisible substance of life fills all space; that its nature is intelligent, plastic, subjective substance.

Five o'clock in the morning is the best time to go into this sort of meditation. If you will retire early every night for one month, before falling asleep impress firmly upon your subjective mind the affirmation "My Father is the ruler of all the world, and is expressing His directing power through me," you will find that the substance of life takes form in the moulds of your thoughts.

Do not accept the above suggestion simply because it is given to you. Think it over carefully until the impression is made upon your own subconscious mind understandingly. Rise every morning, as was suggested before, at five o'clock, sit in a quiet room in a straight-backed chair, and think out the affirmation of the previous evening, and you will realize and be able to put into practice your princely power with the realization to some extent, at least, that your mind really is a center through which all the creative energy and power there is taking form.

Scientific Prayer:

The Principle Underlying Scientific Prayer

In prayer for a change in condition, physical, mental or financial for yourself or another, bear in mind that the fundamental necessity for the answer to prayer is the understanding of the scientific statement:

"Ask, BELIEVING YOU HAVE ALREADY RECEIVED and you shall receive"

This is not as difficult as it appears on the surface, once you realize that everything has its origin in the mind, and that which you seek outwardly, you already possess. No one can think a thought in the future. Your thought of a thing constitutes its origin.

THEREFORE

The Thought Form of the Thing is already Yours as soon as you think it. Your steady recognition of this Thought Possession causes the thought to concentrate, to condense, to project itself and to assume physical form.

To Get Rich Through Creation

The recognition or conception of new forces of wealth is the loftiest aspiration you can take into your heart, for it assumes and implies the furtherance of all noble aims.

Items to be remembered about Prayer for Yourself or Another: Remember that that which you call treatment or prayer is not, in any sense, hypnotism. It should never be your endeavor to take possession of the mind of another. Remember that it should never be your intention to make yourself believe that which you know to be untrue. You are simply thinking into God or First Cause with the understanding that -

"If a thing is true at all, there is a way in which it is true throughout the Universe." Remember that the Power of Thought works by absolutely scientific principles. These principles are expressed in the language of the statement:

"As a man thinketh in his heart, so is he."

This statement contains a world of wisdom, but man's steady recognition and careful application of the statement itself is required to bring it into practical use.

Remember that the principles involved in being as we think in our heart are elucidated and revealed by the law "As you sow, you shall reap."

Remember that your Freedom to choose just what you will think, just what thought possession you will affirm and claim constitutes God's gift to you.

It shows...

How:

First Cause has endowed every man with the Power and Ability to bring into his personal environment whatever he chooses. Cause and Effect in reference to Getting:

If you plant an ACORN, you get an OAK. If you sow a GRAIN OF CORN, you reap a stalk and MANY Kernels of Corn. You always get the manifestation of that which you consciously or unconsciously AFFIRM and CLAIM, habitually declare and expect, or in other words "AS YOU SOW"

Therefore, sow the seeds of I AM ....I OUGHT....I CAN....I WILL REALIZE that because you ARE you OUGHT, that because you OUGHT, you CAN, that because you CAN, you DO.

The manifestation of this Truth, even in a small degree, gives you the indisputable understanding that DOMINION IS YOUR CHARTER RIGHT You are an Heir of First Cause, endowed with all the power He has. God has given you everything. ALL is yours, and you know that all you have to do is to reach out your mental hand and take it.

This Formula may serve as a pattern to shape your own Prayer or Affirmation into God for the benefit of another or yourself.

If for another, you speak the Christian name of the person you wish to help, then dismiss their personality entirely from your consciousness.

Intensify your thought by meditating upon the fact that there is that in you which finds the way, which is the Truth and is the Life.

You are affirming this fact, believing that since you are thinking this, it is already yours. Having lifted up your feeling to the central idea of this meditation, you examine your own consciousness to see if there is ought which is unlike God. If there is any feeling of fear, worry, malice, envy, hatred, or jealousy, turn back in your meditation to Cleanse your Thought through the affirmation that God's Love and Purity fill all space including your heart and soul. Reconcile your thought with the Love of God, always remembering that

You are made in the Image and Likeness of Love.

Keep this Cleansing thought in mind until you feel that you have freed your consciousness entirely of all thoughts and feelings other than

Love and Unity with all Humanity

Then if denials do not disturb you, deny all that is unlike your desired manifestation. This accomplished, you almost overlay your denial with the affirmative thought that: You are made in the Image and Likeness of God and that you already have your desire fulfilled in its first, its original spiritual or thought-form.

Closing of Prayer:

Prayer as a method of thought is a deliberate use of the Law which gives you the Power of Dominion over everything which tends in any way to hamper your perfect liberty. YOU HAVE BEENGIVEN LIFE THAT YOU MAY ENJOY IT MORE AND MORE FULLY The steady recognition of this Truth makes you declare yourself a PRINCE OF POWER.

You recognize, accept and use this power as A CHILD OF A KING AND HENCE DOMINION IS YOUR BIRTHRIGHT Then when you feel the light of this great Truth flooding your consciousness -open the flood-gates of your soul in Heartfelt Praise that you have the understanding that....THE CREATOR AND HIS CREATION ARE ONE.

Also that the Creator is continually creating through his creation.

Close your treatment in the happy assurance that the Prayer which is fulfilled is not a form of supplication but a steady habitual affirming that The Creator of all Creation is operating Specifically through you, therefore

THE WORK MUST BE PERFECTLY DONE - YOUR MIND IS A CENTER OF DIVINE OPERATION.

Hints for Application and Practice:

For every five minutes given to reading and study of the theories of Mental Science, spend fifteen minutes in the use and application of the knowledge acquired.

1. Spend one minute in every twenty-four hours in conscientiously thinking over the specification that must be observed in order to have your prayers answered.

2. Practice the steady recognition of desirable thought possession for two periods of fifteen minutes each every day. Not only time yourself each period to see how long you can keep a given conception before your mental vision, but also keep a written record of the vividness with which you experience your mental image. Remember that your mental senses are just as varied and trainable as your physical ones.

3. Spend five minutes every day between 12 noon and 1 o'clock with a mental search for new sources of wealth. Chapter 17 Chapter 17 Chapter 17 Chapter 17

THINGS TO REMEMBER

Remember that the greatest Mental Scientist the world has ever known (Jesus Christ, the Man) said all things are possible unto you.

Also the "things I do you can do." Did he tell the truth?

Jesus did not claim to be more divine than you are. He declared the whole human race children of God. By birth he was no 'exception to this rule. The power he possessed was developed through His personal effort. He said you could do the same if you would only believe in yourself. A great idea is valueless unless accompanied by physical action. God gives the idea; man works it out upon the physical plane.

All that is really worthwhile is contentment. Self-command alone can produce it. The soul and body are one. Contentment of mind is contentment of soul, and contentment of soul means contentment of body.

If you wish health, watch your thoughts, not only of your physical being, but your thoughts about everything and everybody. With your will keep them in line with your desire, and outwardly act in accordance with your thoughts, and you will soon realize that all power both over thoughts and conditions has been given to you. You believe in God. Believe in yourself as the physical instrument through which God operates. Absolute dominion is yours when you have sufficient self mastery to conquer the negative tendency of thoughts and actions.

Ask yourself daily: "What is the purpose of the power which put me here?" "How can I work with the purpose for life and liberty in me?"

Upon having decided these questions, endeavor hourly to fulfill them. You are a law unto yourself.

If you have a tendency to overdo anything, eat, drink or blame circumstances for your misfortunes, conquer that tendency with the inward conviction that all power is yours outwardly. Eat less, drink less, blame circumstances less, and the best there is will gradually grow in the place where the worst seemed to be.

Always remember that all is yours to use, as you will. You can if you will: if you will you do.

God the Father blesses you with all He has to give.

Make good Godly use of it.

The reason for greater success when you first began your studies and demonstrations in Mental Science is that your joy and enthusiasm at the simple discovery of the power within was greater than you have been able to put into your understanding later.

With increased understanding put increasing joy and enthusiasm, and the results will correspond

How to Live Life and Love it

Foreword

The purpose of this series of personal-pointer Lessons, which are herein compiled into one volume, is to indicate in a clear, concise way "the natural principles governing the relation between the creative action of all thought-power and material things," i.e., circumstances and conditions.

If these few simple principles are carefully studied, and mastered to your satisfaction, and then put into practical, hourly application, the student will find very soon that it is possible for man to make conscious contact with the Almighty, EverPresent, Never-Failing God; and this just naturally means individual freedom, freedom from every form of limitation and bondage of any nature.

(Read Mark 9:23.) Then try to believe that the Spirit of Life, which is your life also, knows "How to Live Life and Love It."

All the joy Life has to give is yours right now!

Let us start on the highway to unqualified success now. God is our guide.

Your loving companion,
Genevieve Behrend

Chapter 1

LIVE LIFE AND LOVE IT!

MASTER: Let us begin this morning's lesson with the certain knowledge that every living thing really wishes to enjoy Life. Once one really has entered into the true Spirit of Life that one can not help loving to live and is certain to enjoy life.

PUPIL: That is just it. If one could get into the Spirit of Living Life, I am sure one, every one, would enjoy it. But it seems to me that the general run of humanity live in the spirit of death rather than of life. The average person I know is always wishing that he could but at the same time knowing that he can't. That does not seem like really living.

MASTER: Indeed that is not living and people who live in that form of mental action are "the living dead." Let us see if we can not find an easy, logical method of entering into the true Spirit of Life. We know that we must enter into the Spirit of a book, or a picture, or of music, else they are entirely meaningless to us. To really appreciate anything we must share the mental attitude of the creative thought and feeling which brought them into outward form.

PUPIL: Now I am wondering if getting into the spirit of a thing would be getting into the spiritual prototype of the thing we may wish to enjoy. For example, I should very much enjoy a home of my own, a husband and children. Can one really get into the spirit of these good things before one do.

PUPIL: But the matter of the right husband, that seems very difficult for me. First, I am not in the right position to contact men and now I have only two men acquaintances, neither of which I should care to live with in my model home.

MASTER: What you say does not enter into the matter at all. All that the individual does is to place into the Originating Creative Power the QUALITY one wishes to differentiate, just as one plugs into the electric current in the house when one wishes to use it. The light, the heater, the Frigidaire, the fan, the iron, or any other thing one may want to use, all are there. All of the power is already there, too. It is ready and waiting; all that is necessary is your recognition of it and your taking action to utilize it. Your recognition and your desire cause you to make the right contact; and the power that is there does all the rest. The ways and means of your meeting the one and only husband are not your own concern; they form themselves into line automatically as a result of your turning on the correct switch.

PUPIL: Do you mean that it is not necessary for me to do anything to try to meet people? Do I not have to go to parties, or visit friends? Sometimes when I should be much happier at home I go to such places, and do such things, because there is always a chance of meeting the right one there.

MASTER: All of that is entirely unnecessary. The power you have turned on within yourself is an attracting Power, remember! To give you an example: One time when we were in Chicago, living at the Medinah Athletic Club, a young lady came to me with much the same attitude that you express and received the same answer I give here. She was a trained nurse, a graduate of St. Luke's. She was tired of living alone, wished a home, a husband, children. After she had had ten or twelve personal interviews and lessons with me I told her, one morning as she was leaving our apartment, that it would not be necessary for her to come to see me again. She felt sure also that the contact had been made. Our apartment was on the forty-second floor; and as she caught the elevator down she said a "great wave of peace and contentment came over her." In her heart she had the consciousness of love and protection even now. At the thirtyfourth floor the elevator stopped and a young man who was very ill got into the elevator. Almost at once he folded up on the floor, unconscious. The elevator operator knew him since he had an apartment in the building; and the nurse and operator together got the man back to his apartment, into bed, and sent for the house-physician who said that the nurse had done exactly the right thing. In about an hour the man regained consciousness and sent for his own physician who wished to assign a nurse of his own choosing to the case. But the patient insisted on having the nurse who had helped him from the elevator, and kept her in attendance on him until he was fully recovered. Just about six months later patient and nurse were married.

PUPIL: That was certainly a lucky break for her, that she should take just that elevator, at that time. That seems to me like drawing the lucky number on bank-night at the theatre. Of course someone always wins but there is no certainty about it, is there?

MASTER: Really the two positions are not at all parallel; they are not even similar. With the nurse it was not luck at all. Deliberately, consciously, in faith, she had plugged into a circuit of great power within herself, the circuit of Universal Power that we call God, or Life and which did produce a perfect reciprocity of feeling and a certain sense of security, protection, provision, companionship In other words she deliberately "initiated a train of causation directed to her individual purpose," to quote Troward, just as you would attach the cord to your electric-iron if you wished to press clothes. There was no luck in the matter whatsoever; it was purest science manifesting, as it always will and does, in answer to a strong desire scientifically placed. Whether it is plugging in to a circuit of electric energy or tuning in with the Creative Life Principle the procedure is exactly the same.

PUPIL: I am beginning to see the light. But the case you have just told me about still seems rather spectacular and unusual.

MASTER: That is because you have not trained the objective quality of your mind to know that it can always trust the Intelligent Creative Spirit of Life within yourself.

You are letting preconceived ideas, and shallow and false ones, take precedent in your mind over pure, scientific Principle.

You do not feel that you need to know the principles of electricity before you can use your vacuum-cleaner. All we know about electricity is gleaned from what we see it do. The same thing applies to Life. The innermost principles of Life will always remain a profound mystery. But one can, and should, live life to the full in the self and love it.

PUPIL: I am wondering if the nurse "lived happily ever after" with her unusually-acquired husband. And did they have the home and the children she so much desired?

MASTER: The couple have lived very happily together for a number of years now and do have a comfortable home and three children. I shall explain more of that later. The secret of living life and loving this:

First, your feeling towards the livingness of life in you, as well as in all life everywhere, should be to recognize life as Intelligent and to know that when this Intelligence is working through you it does not change its essential nature. It has always been a receptive Power, that is amenable to suggestion, and it is always responsive and creative. This is the basis of Troward's meaning in his words which I use for my own favorite affirmation, and which, quoted, is this: "My mind is a center of divine operation. The divine operation is always for expansion and fuller expression; and this means the production of something beyond what has gone before, something entirely new, not included in past experience though proceeding out of it by an orderly sequence of growth.

Therefore since the Divine can not change its inherent nature it must operate in the same manner in me; consequently in my own special world, of which I am the center, it will move forward to produce new conditions, always in advance of any that have gone before." Once you really plug your individual consciousness into the great power of the Universe the above will be your line of thinking. You will involuntarily look to the Life-Principle in you, not only as the only Creative Energy but also as a directive Power.

That is you will let God determine, through your conscious mind, the actual forms and courses which the conditions for its manifestations will always take in your own individual world. Do remember always that the Originating Spirit of Life (of your life, too) is forever a forming Power. It is for this reason that we should use such great care in the selection of our habitual thoughts and feelings - for create they will, and always.

PUPIL: How may I know, for example, that my true husband is being guided to me, or I to him?

MASTER: By your feeling of certainty, even though outward conditions show no sign of the fact. Still you are sure.

You feel close. You know you are protected.

You feel the influence of love all about you.

You have stimulated these special qualities of Life in your individual world by your having persistently looked to God, knowing that He does manifest in you.

Your mental attitude of faith and trust and expectancy has attracted all the joys of life. You realize that all that Life has to give is present with you now just as all that light has to give is present wherever light is.

PUPIL: Do I understand that if I live as closely as possible in the consciousness of reciprocity of feeling, and know that love is guiding, protecting and providing for me with its abundance, I can attract these qualities of life in the form of a man?

MASTER: Yes. For the house and the home feel protection, shelter, perfect harmony. For the husband feel love and joy; then live in the feeling of these things. Feeling is one of the strongest elements in Life and is also the most responsive.

Chapter 2

THE FINE ART OF GIVING

PUPIL: It seems to me that the pace you are setting here is going to be rather severe discipline for me. But since it is to be for only a few weeks, if I wish, I shall try it. If there is not a big change for the better, both inside and out, at the end of that time, I can stop. N'est-ce pas?

MASTER: Yes, but please do not enter lightly upon this study. And do not seek to cultivate an acquaintance with God for the sake of what you will be able to get from Him. This is a tragic mistake that many people make, and which is difficult for many of them to rectify.

They seek first to get, and promise faithfully that they will then give. But in so doing they have inverted the Spirit's Law of Compensation, which is good, which is as just as it is good, and which is as immutable as it is both good and just.

PUPIL: This sounds interesting. What is this Great Law?

MASTER: The law is that first we must give! And after we have given the gett

PUPIL: But is it enough to just love God with all of our hearts, all of our souls, and all of our minds? Must we not do something about it as well?

MASTER: Certainly we must do something about it. Love without the fruits of Love is dead! If we love God, we will serve Him devotedly, faithfully, happily, continuously.

PUPIL: How best may we serve Him?

MASTER: By giving of ourselves to our fellowman! By giving of ourselves to our neighbors as unto ourselves. A scientist, one like Doctor Walter Reed for example, who gives his very life, and lovingly and gladly, in order to benefit mankind knows the true love of God.

So does the heroic nurse who ministers to afflicted mankind out of sheer love of mankind. So does the self-effacing, selfsacrificing mother, or father, or teacher, or minister.

There are many ways in which one may serve. All do not possess scientific talents, nor healing talents, nor comforting talents. But all do possess something they can give! Some who feel themselves unable to serve directly give of themselves by donating money to worthy causes, and these, too, are serving God because they Love their neighbors and therefore Love Him. Let me give you an example of true love as I personally knew it in a wonderful woman, one of many cases that I know.

PUPIL: Yes, do give us an example. They always help to clarify things, and show us how others have done what we wish to do.

MASTER: Very well. This divine soul was reared in a home of great wealth and culture. But as a very young woman she made up her mind to go out into the world, "on the firing-line" itself, as she called it, to serve actively lovingly, there. She became a nun, and as such was assigned to a hospital as a trained nurse. As she entered upon her lifework she was filled with love for mankind, with enthusiasm for serving God by serving his suffering ones. And she did serve lovingly, happily, faithfully, tenderly eight hours a day, or even twelve hours daily. But the hospital was woefully understaffed; and Marie, as we shall call her here, was soon subject to call sixteen hours daily; and even during the eight hours when she was supposed to have her rest she was often summoned and asked to serve more. Her quarters were right on the same floor with many of the patients, and this ward was her charge day and night. Often at two or three o'clock in the morning the bell beside her bed would ring with an urgent summons. She would arise at once, go to the patient and minister to his or her wants. But in due time she became physically tired, and of course she began to resent the calls that broke into her rest, especially when it seemed to her, as it often did at these times, that the patient merely wished a drink of water, or wanted a pillow adjusted a certain way, or was merely lonely, all of which were irritating trifles to a weary nurse.

For a month or more these trials went on, seemingly from bad to worse. Marie resolved almost desperately to do something about it, and immediately. So she cast about for a way to best remedy the situation. For days she thought about the matter, asking the Spirit for guidance. At length the flash came, directly from the Infinite! She took up a little card, wrote down the new motto that had been given her, and fastened it on the wall above her bed, right by the service bell, so that she might see it and be again reminded every time the buzzer rang. On the card she had written: "The master calls!" Of course her system worked from the beginning. Quite soon she was saying in immediate answer to the bell, even while sleepily fumbling for her light: "The master calls!" And she would arise and go and serve, without impatience, without resentment, yes, rejoicing in the opportunity to again serve in love.

As a consequence her energy was untiring; she easily and joyfully did the work of three nurses, always rested, always fresh, always efficient, always smiling, whenever called. Her patients loved her greatly. She was always cheerful, always encouraging, always aglow, as it were, with a holy Love. And to those who did not know her secret, as very few did, the patients she attended seemed to be "miraculously healed." Let your motto also be: "The master calls!" And remember that the humblest service that you can render to the lowliest of your fellowmen, if rendered in LOVE, is a direct service to Him!

PUPIL: This is a profoundly beautiful and powerful illustration. Is that the motto, or the principle, that you use in helping the many who come to you? If not, what is your own personal secret of serving?

MASTER: My own method, in a way, is very similar to that of Marie. Like her I wished to serve lovingly, to serve as many as possible, to help to the limit of my powers in alleviating any and all kinds of suffering, physical, mental, spiritual or other form of unhappiness . Not only do I strive always to help those who seek me out. Every person whose hand I take into mine in greeting, every person into whose eyes I look, in all places at all times, yes even the shop girl who sells me my hose, the milkman who comes to my door, the beggar on the street, everyone to whom

I speak at any and all times receives the same strong spiritual impulse from me! I INTENTIONALLY SEE THE RADIANT CHRIST IN ALL!

PUPIL: But I thought that you told me once you never mentally treat people unless they ask for help.

MASTER: I don't, not specifically, not specifically under any other circumstances. My secret is this: I have deliberately formed the habit of beholding the Christ in every soul that my eyes fall upon! I do not ever see anyone as being poor, or old, or ill, or bereaved, or lonely, or homely, or evil or imperfect in any way. I behold each and all as only perfect! I see only the Radiant Christ in every one of them because the christ is in each of them!

Chapter 3

THE ART OF RECIPROCITY

MASTER: The Bible, the sages of all time, all sources of real truth, unite in ab-solute agreement concerning one great thing, namely: That God and Man are one and not two, that the "two" are not separated but indissolubly joined in perfect and harmonious union.

The Invisible (Spirit) and the visible (form, or matter) actually ARE inseverably connected. Each is a complement of the other.

And the whole of Truth is to be found only in the combination of the "two," which really are not "two" but one through eternal union!

PUPIL: I am particularly happy about this conclusion because I used to think that a person could not have both spiritual and physical blessings at one and the same time. I thought that the physical world had nothing of God in it. Yes, I thought that Spirit was utterly separated from form, or matter. Now I feel sure that the reason I did not make any real progress then was that I was trying to have an inside for Life without an outside, and an outside without any inside. In other words I was simply living in the physical world without being conscious of the fact that forever I have a direct connection with the Spiritual Realm. I am right, am I not, in believing and feeling that I must have the realization that each is vitally necessary to the other for the formation of a Substantial Entity.

MASTER: Yes, you are exactly right! No one can go very far on the great highway of Truth until he realizes that there never was, and never will be, an inside to anything without an outside also. While one is visible and the other invisible (to the human eye) the only reality is in the combination of the two. A constant awareness of this fact on our part brings us that radiant realization of one-ness, of union, that we must have if we hope to make any progress in Truth.

PUPIL: After this one basic realization what other truths must we have?

MASTER: We must know that underlying the totality of all things is the source of all things, the Great Cosmic Intelligence. We must know that no physical thing of itself only can ever create anything. The physical form is the instrument that Life (God) fashioned of His own Essence in order to have something through which He could work His wonders, and give them form also. But He always lives in that instrument! Do not ever lose sight of this fact: The power is always greater than the form through which it manifests, just as electricity is infinitely greater than the bulb through which it manifests as light. It is through union of forms, positive with negative, or masculine with feminine, or Spirit with Soul, that the creation of all forms, or channels, or physical things, results. This eternal principle runs all through the Bible, is the warp and woof of it, the whole substance of it. Seek ye the answer in that Great Book!

PUPIL: But many people say that the Bible is "antiquated," that it is a "book of fables," and of "old wives' tales," etc.

MASTER: How does this concern YOU? Which is the more reliable guide, do you think, the spiritually darkened ones who criticised the Bible or thine own soul which knows light when it sees it? Are you going to do your own thinking or shall you be content to let others do it for you, and wrongly? If we must go to other people in our quest of Truth, let us resolve to go to ones who have the light of the Spirit.

For instance, what does Troward say of the Bible? Let his Wisdom be our guide here. He tells us that "the Bible is the Book of the emancipation of man!" He adds that this means man's complete "deliverance from sorrow, sickness, poverty, struggle, uncertainty, from ignorance and limitation, and finally from death itself." This noble conception of Troward's is exactly what the Bible IS. With such a wonderful Book in print one should not be surprised to learn that it has the widest circulation of any book ever published, that it is still the world's best seller. If the Bible were not Truth, it would not live through so many generations and still hold its pre-eminent position. So let us proceed on the assumption that Troward is right, that the Bible DOES contain the secret whereby the art of living a perfectly free and happy life may be attained.

PUPIL: But the Bible has never been a very interesting book to me. I have thought of it as "old world fables."

MASTER: It was uninteresting to you because you did not understand it. Nevertheless it is a most scientific Book, full of interesting facts and life giving Truth, the finest book ever written about the greatest of all the sciences, the Science of life.

PUPIL: My parents were religious people, church every Sunday morning, prayers every day, and all of that. But I could never see that they were any better off, or any happier -if as happy -than the neighbors who never went to church. But I shall be glad to make an honest effort to understand and follow whatever you outline, even the Bible if you say so.

MASTER: I have spoken. And because you are honest in your desire you will be honest in your thinking; and honest thinking makes a true student. Because you truly wish to understand the art of living you shall come to know it, and when you know Life and really live it you are certain to love it. The Bible IS, I repeat the book of life, and of Life's immutable Laws. Remember always that Life's Laws contain within themselves the solution to every human problem! Indeed "Wisdom is the beginning of magic." The Spirit of Christ, or Intelligent Life, within us is the light of each of us. It will always make the path easy, interesting and joyous IF only we will study and understand how to use our own Divine Power, and then really use it. Once one has formed the habit of looking to the Bible for the answer to all problems it becomes to that one as a lantern carried on a dark night.

The next steps ahead may be in total darkness, but when you approach the light you carry illuminates the path and you know exactly where to step, and just what to do. Your feeling is influenced in the right direction. It is true that the Bible veils its most profound secrets in symbols and parables; but the Wisdom is there for the earnest and consecrated seeker!

Maybe, the author, was right when he wrote:

"The true artist finds that the materials for his art are ever present. But the ones who can discern the possible uses of these varied materials, and who possess the instinct, intuition and training to put them to their best uses are always few in number. The materials out of which art is made are ever present; but the artist appears only at intervals!"

So it is with the mysterious force we call Life. Every person has it; but the ones who understand and use Life's finest possibilities, and who get out of it, consequently, its very richest growth are really very few in number. So let us put into this study of Life our very noblest personal energy.

PUPIL: It seems to me, judging from what you say here and from what you have already taught us in these lessons, that our perfecting of the art of living and loving it is based upon the training of the mind and feeling to the point where we shall find as much joy and satisfaction in self-discipline as we formerly found in self-indulgences. Am I right?

MASTER: Yes. Once one has gone that far on the path, he is then around the last turn and on the "way that is straight," the path of splendor that leads directly to conscious union with the father! The Bible says the art of really living and loving Life centers around the record of man's thoughts and feelings, his aspirations, inspirations and experiences, on his discovery of the Life-Spirit as "an ever present help in trouble." When a man has found his real self (the God-Self, or Christ-Radiance) within, when he has discovered the infinite possibilities and potentialities with which he is forever surrounded, when he lives these things and loves the life he lives he becomes the true artist! Then will he use the right materials, then will he produce the results desired in the form of the picture that he originally conceived!

PUPIL: Suppose one has never had the advantages of higher education, that one's whole life has been commonplace and restricted, would such a one be able to understand and apply these beautiful and interesting truths?

MASTER: Yes indeed! One's station in life does not make the slightest difference. One may be a woman who is trying to cook a good meal in the one and only room that she has, on a one-burner gasstove. One may be a man who is a shoe-salesman, and who spends his whole time every day trying to satisfy women customers who insist upon his trying to perfectly and comfortably fit dainty shoes to their large feet.

One may be a king or queen or a servant or a pauper. High or low, exalted or humble, man is a spiritual being! So long as he can think he can always change the outer, or physical, effects to suit the desire of his heart. And the very first steps lie in the thought and in the feeling!

PUPIL: When one's whole environment is one of poverty, or illness, or other dark limitations, how can one have beautiful and hopeful thoughts? Is it not true that the environment influences one's thoughts and feelings? While one is forced to live in the same adverse environment I do not see how there can be much change.

MASTER: If one were perfectly satisfied with an environment such as you describe there could not, and would not, be any change. But if one were divinely dissatisfied with such conditions, and very much wished to change them, it may be done any time, as completely as one may wish, by resort to and use of the Laws of Life.

Suppose, for example, that you would like a position that is more agreeable, more lucrative, shorter hours, etc. If you go forth to look for such a "job," by all means start out with the feeling that you have something valuable to give an employer, and not go out to see how much you can get. If you give the getting will automatically follow. Carry the light of God-consciousness with you in seeking betterment of your position; and when you approach your prospective employer let the light shine.

Suppose too, that you wish a better, more comfortable house in which to live. The very fact that you desire this change is proof positive that it is for you to have if you will meet the requirements. Many persons try to bring harmony into a home by getting a larger and better home, or by changing companions, by moving into another community.

PUPIL: That would help, would it not?

MASTER: Temporarily it might. But it would in no sense endure. To attempt to bring happiness or freedom into one's life through outward changes only is not wisdom, is not true art. Such is misuse of the divine materials. The change must occur within, and within first! It must first be established in mind, and firmly enthroned there if it is to be other than only temporarily effective. As long as a trend of thought remains the same the result will be the same. The law of life is: To change an effect the cause must be changed first. Cause leads; effects follow! Thought is the cause; conditions are the effects!

PUPIL: Does one's longing for beautiful surroundings, for health and freedom, for a lovely picture in perfect balance, come from the Great Artist who has made all of Nature? Is it He painting His ideal picture for us on the canvas of our individual minds?

MASTER: Yes, God is Mind, Life, Intelligence, Power, Beauty, Love, Harmony, etc. If any of these things are desired by us, and they are, then surely the Creator of them all must have planted that thought-seed in the mind. He must have whispered into that mental ear and that spiritual heart that the truth is yours! God has chosen you as a holy instrument through which to manifest all of His beautiful and wonderful qualities of Life. It is the divine order and will that you should manifest that particular thing, that particular place in Life!

Chapter 4

GOD-CONSCIOUSNESS VERSUS SENSE-CONSCIOUSNESS

PUPIL: Then if our truly fine desires are the desires of God Himself trying to manifest in and through us as individuals, in some particular way, why are there so many misfits in life? Why are there so very few who are doing, really doing, just what they would like to do? Why are there so very, very few living the life they truly wish to live? Why? Why? Why? Surely God can fulfill His own desires.

MASTER: Unless all things are possible to God then nothing is possible to Him. God has projected each human forth from Himself, each of us possessing an individual mind, for the sole purpose of manifesting Himself and His glory through us. Verily the mind of man is the son of God! The Son has been given absolute liberty. Each can always make of his life, for a time at least, whatsoever he may choose.

Man already possesses everything that God had to give him!

Each person can make or mar his own picture, exactly as he wishes. By nature man is free to draw from the Ever-Present Parent Mind anything, and all things, that he requires to fulfill his desires. If this is not true then God's highest creation, man, is a mere nothing, an automatic something like a clock which when once wound will run until it runs down. Man IS, however, God's own idea in flesh. The Intelligent Life in man is man's Divine Father! Man is already perfect and complete, IS made of the same essence as his Father (God)!

There is only one reason why every mortal does not manifest and reproduce the Life, Love and Beauty which we see brought out in such radiance and perfection in all of Nature, manifested in Nature to the extreme point where mechanical and automatic actions can bring them. But we as individuals have a Law of Being that is somewhat different in one way from that which governs the other creatures that are of the world we call Nature. For us that are human the only perfect reproduction of Life, Love, Power and Beauty that we can ever know must come from Liberty. That is to say we have freedom of choice that is commensurate with that of the Originating Life-Spirit Itself. In other words we as individuals have the liberty of accepting or rejecting either good or evil, exactly as we may choose them. And the choice that we make results from the state of our consciousness. If we are God-conscious, we are gods. But if we are sense-conscious only, then we are creatures of darkness, of illness, of poverty, of loneliness, and all other things that are undesirable. "Choose ye well, therefore, whom ye will serve!" God-consciousness or sense-consciousness, which?

PUPIL: You have given us a powerful and illuminating "dose" here. Already we have a whole lesson. But I still do not see why God's highest creation, man should ever reject any of the good things of life.

MASTER: IF man really understood the Law of his own Being, he never should reject the good things. But there are few who fully understand this Law, which is a wide-open door to absolute freedom! Most people believe that the "law of their being" (purposely spelled without capital letters) is a law of limitation rather than a law of absolute liberty!

Man "does not expect to find the starting point of the Creative Process reproduced in himself; so he looks to the mechanical side of things for the basis of his reasoning about Life. Consequently his reasoning leads him to the conclusion that Life is limited because he has assumed limitation as his premise; and so, logically, he can not escape from it (limitation) in his conclusion."

Here in this wonderful quotation from Troward you have the whole story of limitation. Here Troward shows most clearly that is all a matter of consciousness! And so the tragedy results because man in his dense ignorance ridicules the idea of transcending the law of limitation, forgetting completely (if indeed he ever learned it) that the law can include all of the lower laws so fully as to completely swallow them!

PUPIL: From what you say it would seem that man's only reason for knowing limitation of any kind is his own lack of understanding. Is man to blame because he does not know?

MASTER: No man is to blame for what he does not know. But surely all persons will suffer because of not using what they do know! And they shall keep right on suffering until, like small children, they learn from experience.

PUPIL: It seems "strange," to say the least, that each of us must learn to find his own fuller Life in his own way. Why did not God compel His idea (man) to understand from birth that Life is Joy, and Joy is Freedom, etc...?

MASTER: Please think for just a minute! Would there be any freedom, any liberty, in that kind of person? Such an individual should be a mere automaton with no sense of liberty at all! God forbid that any of us, His children, become robots!

PUPIL: It seems to me that most people feel life is entirely made up of a constant round of prosaic and homely activities which we are obliged to follow: To the shop, or office we go. We toil and slave, and go home again, all worn out and cranky. We sleep, maybe, then arise to repeat it all again for years until in God's mercy we die. There can be no real joy in that kind of life; but to most of mankind that is all. Still this is not all, is it?

MASTER: Indeed that is not all, not even for the darkest and most limited of persons. However dark, spiritually and materially, a person may be, deep down in his soul there is a conviction that Life holds his desires fulfilled somehow, somewhere, sometime! He feels also that if he only knew how he could find a way! Some feel that the real joy of liberty can come only after putting off the body at death. this is not the case, however, everything that life (god) has to give is here in our midst, and right now!

As we humans advance in knowledge, either from study or experience, or both, we overcome one law of limitation after another by finding the higher and greater law of which all lower laws are but partial expressions.

At length we see clearly before us, as our ultimate goal, this Truth:

> "Nothing less than the perfect law of liberty
> -not liberty without Law, which is anarchy
> -but liberty according to law!"

When man learns the Law of his own Being, he will specialize it in all of his ways and will have found his true place. Thus will he bring into form all of the desires of his heart; then will he know the real art of living!

PUPIL: Can anyone who will learn from Life, either by study or experience, that the Creative Energy, with ALL that it has to give, is an Ever-Present, Responsive Quality of Life? Then can one really materialize, really bring into outward form, his most secret and sacred desires! That would be the art of living sure enough.

MASTER: the law of life is changeless forever! It is always calling to you in these words, or in ones like them:

"Come unto me! Learn about me! Through me all things are possible unto you because we, you and I, are eternally one!

I am life! I am Creative;

I am always Responsive to the thoughts and emotions with which I am impressed by you!

I am mind!

The Law of Mind is my law!

Because this is true it is Truth also that 'as you think in your heart so are you!'

Thinking gives form to the unformed Life!"

PUPIL: This is splendid! But again it is getting "heavy." May we have another personal illustration of the adaptation of this principle to everyday living as people live it? This will help, I am sure.

MASTER: All right; I am always happy to comply with such requests if they will really help you.

I once knew a dentist, a very fine dentist and a good man. He confided to me one day that music was his very life, and not prosaic dentistry. He said that he was weary of being "down in the mouth all of the time."

"So," I asked, "you feel that you are not in your right place?"

"I know that I am not!" he replied.

"Just why aren't you in your right groove?" I queried.

"Because music will not yield me enough money to keep my family in anything like moderate comfort. I feel that marriage and a family are among Life's deepest joys and greatest blessings. But music is like politics; one has to have lots of 'pull' to get into the few places that will really pay for a good violinist."

"Are you sure of that?" I asked.

"Yes, quite!"

"Well, Mr. Dentist," I said, "I know a God who is All-Intelligent, All-Powerful, Ever-present, Ever-Responsive and Forever Creative! He is also the Greatest of Master Artists, the Real Maestro! He lives forever deep within your own soul. If you will try going into Him there, if you will establish Harmony there, and will know and understand the Beauty which your music must express there, and if you will be content only with perfection there and in your music, I know that you can and will reap all the reward that any one can wish for in music, just as in any other profession, art or business."

"Your words cause my hopes to soar," he said. "But how can one like me, one who knows very little about God, contact Him?"

"Go within yourself! Go through, or beneath, the confusing, bewildering, disheartening past experiences. Live wholly in and enjoy only the harmonious side of your nature, which is wise, beautiful and most powerful in all ways. Then practice, practice, practice putting that INNER Beauty and Harmony into vibration through the strings of your violin."

"But I am too old to take this up now."

"Not at all! Loving music as you do, you have kept up with your practice, have you not? Then do try what i have told you!

Try it with faith and love in your heart. Hold them there with a determination and pride which simply will not surrender."

The dentist continued to find excuses, many of them, like so many people do, tragically enough. He did not have time, nor did he feel like it, after long, hard days at the office. He should have to give some time to his family, must have some recreation, etc., etc. But I did not hear him. I kept right on singing glowing word-notes for him, tempting him to try hard, inspiring him with courage.

When he stopped finding excuses, and seemed really interested, he asked for the exact method to use.

I told him the following steps:

(1) First, he must thoroughly make up his mind that his love for music, his deep passion for the expression of harmony was no accident; he must know that it was nothing less than God Himself persistently, relentlessly urging for expression through him.

(2) He should go carefully over and recite to himself the Lord's prayer, quietly but with much love and feeling, not less than twice every day, each night upon retiring and each morning when he first awakened.

(3) He should faithfully visualize himself playing, playing, playing, joyfully, harmoniously, enthusiastically playing to large and most appreciative audiences, receiving really handsome checks for his concerts, etc.

(4) After his periods of visualizing he should faithfully use some affirmation that appealed to him, that would strengthen his faith when it sagged, that would feed his high resolve, that would fan his burning urge to a holy flame.

(5) He should practice, practice, practice his music, striving always with all of his heart and soul to do much better with each rendition than he had ever done before.

Within less than one year the dentist became the musician! He was making more from his "pot boiler" concerts than he had ever made at dentistry. Within another half-year he began a national concert-tour which within a few months yielded him enough to go to Europe for additional study for two years, and to have his family with him over there. Since that time he has done nothing, professionally, but play his violin. He has not, of course, accumulated a really great fortune, but he and his loved ones have all of the good things of life that they wish, and this, combined with an abiding sense of happiness, constitutes true wealth for any person!

PUPIL: Does this same plan apply to everyone, and the same steps?

MASTER: The same principles apply to all!

The exact plan, and the steps that lead to its fulfillment, will vary a little, of course, with each specific case. But no matter what your big desire may be, your Father's dearest wish for you is the absolute fulfillment of that desire by you, by you in partnership with Him!

He always longs to give you any and all good things! His whole purpose in having created you was that He might express himself through you!

This is exactly why he created individuals, and this is why he does live in and through them!

If we would have any of His gifts as our very own we need only to lift up our fallen consciousness to this holy belief and then work in sheer joy and expectation towards the lovely vision we have in view!

Chapter 5

PERSONAL INTIMACY WITH GOD

PUPIL: Please tell me a definite way to get closer to God, to push the little love and understanding that I have further into the Great One-ness until my limited vision is completely absorbed in the Unlimited. Will you do this just for me?

MASTER: Gladly. Since this is your own book, you may take all the time that you require, and at such intervals as you please, to study it, then study it still some more, and to practice it until you have really mastered it and made it a part of your very self. The very best way to completely sublimate your human self, your sense self with all of its limitations, into the infinite is to establish within yourself a personal intimacy with God!

PUPIL: But can this be done? Do you mean to say that we may actually be on terms of personal intimacy with God, as with a friend or other loved one? Such a thing seems too good to be true, too strange and mysterious to believe.

MASTER: Yes, this can be done. In fact it is done in each of us at all times whether or not we are aware of it. Remember always that each of us was made by, and out of the same stuff as, the Ever-Present, Intelligent, Creative Life Itself Each of us was fashioned out of It Itself; and each of us IS It Itself in a physical form.

This being so, it automatically follows that each of us is always in a most personal intimacy with God! God IS our Maker, our very life, our body, our thoughts, our desires, our everything!

PUPIL: Then why are there any troubles at all in this world? Why is not the lot of every person peace, joy and perfection at all times?

MASTER: That question I have answered a number of times, in one form or another. But yet once again let me say that it is all a matter of each individual's own consciousness.

Our thoughts make us what we are!

The whole shape of our lives, and of what we call "conditions," take their form from our most habitual thought and feeling!

Don't ever lose sight of this outstandingly important fact.

The Originating Creative Power is unformed relative to your individual life until it flows through your thought! It is through out constant awareness of the truth that God IS ever-resident within us, IS forever flowing through us as thought, that we are lifted right out of the old, limited habits of judging everything from external appearances, or from sense-consciousness only.

PUPIL: But I still do not quite see how this awareness will change the whole life from darkness to light. Just how will it do it?

MASTER: If you are constantly aware of the fact that you really are God himself in miniature, that you ARE always on terms of personal intimacy with Him as with your own self, then you will not any longer think thoughts that are unlike Him.

You will not think thoughts of limitation of any nature; you will not judge anything or anybody from the standpoint of sense-consciousness.

And when you have changed your Thoughts and Feelings to the point where you are habitually thinking only from the spiritual side of things you will readily discover that to really know god is to be God!

Then indeed are you in constant personal intimacy with God; and you will leave far behind you the dismal bogs of failure, lack, disease, loneliness and despair. You will emerge into, and abide securely in, the green pastures of the fulfillment of your every treasured desire! Persist, persist and yet again persist, in your steady recognition of the Truth that the actual purpose of the Divine in having projected YOU into being from its own Bosom was this and this only: That it might continually flow through you as consciousness, and that it might always specialize in you as health, wealth, peace and joy!

Through this realization you lift your thought and feeling above limitations, and this is the solution to every problem. Yes, through the radiant gate of personal intimacy with God we step into a new world in which all is life and liberty! Truly God is an ever-present everywhere all-the-time, loving, responsive, creative power!

PUPIL: Since you often encourage us to use the Bible as a standard and a way-shower, can you refer us to a place in the Bible in which we are given a means of establishing this conscious personal intimacy with God?

MASTER: Certainly. The Bible is replete with illustrations of this very principle.

For instance, let's turn to St. Matthew, Chapter 22, verses 36, 37, 38, 39 and 40; and note what Jesus, the Greatest of all Great Teachers, says there. Let us study it and analyze it carefully.

Here it is:

(a) Verse 36: "Master, what is the great commandment in the Law?" This question, asked of Jesus by the

lawyer, was one of vital importance; and in the answer that Jesus gave is the golden key that millions desire.

Note the reply below:

(b) Verses 37 and 38: "Jesus said unto him: 'Thou shalt love the Lord thy God with all thy heart, and with all thy soul, and with all thy mind! This is the first and great commandment."

Kindly note very carefully, and ponder deeply, the three steps that are united into one through His use of the word "love."

The heart, the soul and the mind constitute all of the spiritual being!

Hence if we really love God with all of our heart and soul and mind, we are in fact loving Him with all of our all! Is this not true? Indeed it is!

Here then we have Jesus' own way, His own method, of establishing within Himself personal intimacy with God!

(c) Verses 39 and 40 read thus: "And the second (commandment) is like unto it (like unto the first one) Thou shalt love thy neighbor as thyself! On these two commandments hang all the law and the prophets."

Please observe here the tremendous importance that Jesus places upon loving our neighbors as we love our own selves. There are many who pay lip service to this Divine injunction, and who profess that they really DO love their neighbors as themselves. But when it comes to the crucial test of dividing their possessions in love with a less fortunate neighbor, or of going to any extremity of "trouble" for him, their protestations of love for the neighbors are far too often found to be only mere words, shallow and empty and vain. So remember this: in words without deeds to support them there is no virtue! It is a fact that our neighbors (every last one of them) are as precious in the sight of God as we are; in truth our neighbors are an integral part of ourselves, in other forms.

It is a fact also that we can not really love God unless we love our neighbor; and it is a still greater truth that if we do love our neighbor as we love our self we are loving God.

God is ONE!

Yet most of us make the tragic mistake of thinking that God is many, that our neighbor is one person and we another, etc.

The divine reality, however, is that all people (yes every last one of the millions and millions on earth) are one body unified forever in GOD! This being so, it is impossible for us to help a neighbor (who is our self) without also helping ourselves.

Neither can we criticize, condemn or injure a neighbor (who is our self) without doing ourselves greater harm than is done to the neighbor. In personal intimacy with God there is, in reality no "neighbor" and no "self," as two persons, as ones separate and apart from each other; rather each of us is also all other persons, and all other persons are our own selves! When the dwellers on earth learn this all-important lesson that Jesus taught, and when all persons are obedient to this Law, then we shall have the Millennium here in our midst -then will all of us be veritable angels of the one divine body!

PUPIL: This is a most beautiful and powerful illustration. In addition to studying about it and thinking about it what else should we do about it?

MASTER: The most important thing of all is to practice it, to live it!

Otherwise there is no virtue in it at all.

If you can accept these words of Jesus as Truth, then ally yourself with them in your thought and feeling and actions, then will your whole being be fed with spiritual Manna.

You will be given constant suggestions by the Spirit regarding the sanest and most fruitful methods of living your own personal life in true unity with GOD.

PUPIL: And will this not develop still more in us that great essential to which you gave such importance in Lesson Number One, namely a good disposition?

MASTER: Indeed it will! And no age in all of history has ever more needed to learn and practice this great lesson of growth, development and true enrichment than the people of today. Many read the Truth; few assimilate it!

Many hear the Truth; few heed it!

Many know the Truth; few do it!

That is exactly why there is a real master only at long and rare intervals.

The price of mastery is really easy; but it is so much contrary to sense-consciousness (out of which all selfishness is born) that FEW have the courage, the faith and the spiritual stamina, and the LOVE, to try it earnestly, or to stick to it through outward confusion, until it has been proved!

PUPIL: Is there any other method you can think of that will help us to understand this Great Law still better? Are there any short cuts? In the study I mean, not in the practice of it?

MASTER: Yes, there are short-cuts from which a truly observant and intelligent person may find this Law actually fulfilled in beautiful harmony, and from which we humans may learn a very great deal, if we will. Perhaps the greatest of these shortcuts to illumination is the one that is most widely distributed, and to which every last soul has access in one form or another, and with very little "trouble" if they sincerely wish to seek it out. I mean nature, of course.

All of Nature shows forth the glory of living in constant personal intimacy with GOD! By way of example of what I mean, let us briefly study the four seasons of the year, and the reaction of Nature to each. Spring in all of Nature is the period of immortality expressed anew, and in wonderful splendor! It is the season of budding, of flowering, of mating, of Generation and of Re-generation, all of which are among the holiest of the functions of Nature.

And mark well how all of Dame Nature's children are always obedient to the urge of Spring, to the sublime song of the Spirit! Only men are rebellious to the holy commands of the Spirit; and it appears quite obvious that only men sin. How long will it be before we who are human awaken to the true glory that is our divine birthright?

In the realm of Nature summer is the time when fruits are formed, developed and ripened in fulfillment of the Law of the Spirit.

It is the season when seeds are formed within the fruits so that with the coming of another spring all of Nature may obey again the great injunction found so often in the account of Creation in Genesis, namely; "Be ye fruitful and multiply, and fill the face of the earth with fruit." With the autumn comes the precious harvest, the time when the radiant promise that was given in the spring is fulfilled in form, just as every promise of the Spirit to US will surely be manifested in form in our lives, and with a most bountiful harvest, IF only we humans will learn to OBEY the Spirit without question, as do the fair children of Nature, and cease our foolish rebellion that is the one and only source of all of our afflictions!

Then follows the winter and Nature rests from its labors of the spring, summer and fall, just as we also must have our periods of rest. But winter positively is not aging, or decadence, or death, not in Nature. It is the season of rest, of slumber, only. But if you want to think that winter is the symbol of "death," as some people insist upon doing, I will agree with you for a minute solely for the purpose of pointing out the fallacy of death, or the belief in death, as clearly revealed by Nature.

In winter Nature does appear dead. But is it dead? By no means! With the first few warm days of spring the life which has been merely somnolent in Nature, (but which has not perished because it can not perish, not ever) again responds! The buds, animated anew by the vitality of the Spirit, swell and burst; and the leaves and flowers that were hidden from view (but there nevertheless) come harmoniously, joyously forth in their beauty and glory to express immortality! As Nature does so may man do also if he only will. If you would know true illumination, and the power and the glory that are born of it, go thou to nature! Study her ways and be wise! Study her ways and really live!

Chapter 6

INDIVIDUALITY

(What Is the Truth about the Individual and His Individuality?)

MASTER: Have you ever given thought to the matter of how you came into existence?

Are you convinced that there was, and is, a definite purpose in the Divine Mind to account for your being here on earth?

Or do you think that you create the purpose of your life for yourself, independently of all other factors, after you come into this world?

PUPIL: You ask questions that I scarcely know how to answer. These questions have perhaps been of mild and brief interest to me in the past; but I have never given them any real thought. I have let my mind wander as concerns these points. One time I would think that the Creative Parent Mind does have a definite purpose in my being here, and that this being so there is no use in my trying to change things. But it would then occur to me that this conception of things would mean the "pre-destination" of the fundamentalists. So I would change my mind and decide that I must have some hand in determining my mental and spiritual progress. Is this right?

MASTER: Indeed you do have a hand in your self-development. You have a very great part in it! The life that is you as an individual came directly out of the Great Whole of Intelligent Life (God), from out of its very own sacred heart-center.

Your very life is the Spirit's gift of its own self to you! Secondly, the Divine did have a specific purpose in having made you namely: That it might have a new form, a new center, through which it might operate as thought and feeling, and through which it might yet more fully enjoy itself in a particular way.

This also is the Spirit's gift of its own self to you! But the manner in which you as an individual use these holy gifts is left entirely in your hands, without interference from the Spirit.

You were given other holy boons; you were given initiative and selection; you were given absolute freedom of choice!

The distance that you travel towards the goal of spiritual perfection in this earth life depends solely upon you, just as the degree of rapidity with which you may mentally grow is entirely up to you!

PUPIL: But are we not given certain divine urges, or longings at all stages of our lives which will help us to know the right way to go? Are we not given these certain desires, or impulses, or stimuli?

MASTER: Certainly. And unless one follows these Divine impulses one is never really quite satisfied, one is always restless, always feels that some essential is lacking, that his right place eludes him.

Your very individuality is an exact complement of the Great Whole, is a specialized action of all of Life. The only difference in the Life, the Love, the Beauty or the Power of the Universal (God) and of the individual (man), as expressed through the Universal and the individual, is a difference in scale. The quality of the two (which in reality are but one) is exactly the same! The very same Creator who made and directs the whole universe also made and will direct you, if you will let Him do so, because He himself lives in you as the Life of you. His infinite Creative Power and Intelligent Love are the very same in you that they are in all other created things. Therefore it is not just sentiment to say and feel and know, as did Jesus: 'The Father (God) and I are One! the Father in me, He doeth the work!"

If only we will develop a constant recognition of this most profound Truth, we shall then really have an abiding sense of liberty, of liberty in union, of liberty in conscious union with all of life! This is not just an idle but beautiful rhapsody; it is a simple, but most powerful and illuminating, statement of fact!

PUPIL: Am I right then in believing that if I could really think myself into an unshakable conviction that God IS everpresent in me, and that all of His Creative Power is mine to draw from at my own will and pleasure, I could accomplish anything and everything that i might wish, and could be and have whatsoever I might desire?

MASTER: Yes, you are right. The Creative Power of God in us is unformed with respect to what we may wish to accomplish until we ourselves give it definite direction with our thought and feeling. It is always responsive, remember, to any and all of our thoughts and feelings. These things being true, and they are true, any person may BE, do and have whatsoever that one may desire, if, of course, one actively works in a corresponding direction.

It is logic, it is purest gospel, that there is no other way than the one that Life's true purpose in us is to be forever seeking to express itself through us as freedom! Remember always, I urge you, that our thoughts and feelings do become things, and that they determine the shape that the unformed substance of the Spirit takes in its living expression in our individual lives.

It is, as Troward says, like water flowing through a pipe; the water always assumes the shape and the size of the pipe through which it is sent.

It is like harnessed electricity which always manifests in exact correspondence with the kind of instrument through which it passes as it works. In the light-bulb the electricity actually becomes light; in the doorbell it rings the bell; in the refrigerator it generates cold; in the stove it becomes heat. It is the same electricity, the same Power, in every case; and the instrument through which it passes determines what the Power is and what it does!

Once a person truly grasps the real meaning of the Spirit's Principles, then one realizes fully that we as individuals are actually sent out from the very Heart of God Himself in order that we may become and be new and perfect centers through which He can operate in joy, in ever-increasing joy.

This and this only, is the will of God towards us! Yes, the exalted mission of each of us is that we may be new instruments for divine expression. If we will to become that, and will make the necessary mental and physical effort to realize this Truth, then we will know that we are filling our right place in life. we shall experience true and lasting happiness then because we shall be doing the things we most enjoy doing. There will be an ever present-sense of growth in our lives also.

Only a very few individuals have ever reached this empyrean height in consciousness while on the earth-plane; still it is possible to all. Because so few attain this exalted level most people have the merest existence, one that is filled with seemingly continual and perplexing problems of one sort or another.

PUPIL: It seems to me there are many more people who are unhappy here than happy ones. So many of my personal friends feel themselves to be misfits in life, I do not think that I know even one person, including myself, who is perfectly happy. If one has health, as some do, then that one may have financial troubles. If they do not have financial worries, and no real physical woes, then they have family discord. And so on it goes until one wonders if there is such a thing as complete happiness in this phase of existence.

MASTER: You are right; and the real reason for all of this unrest is this: These individuals have not recognized that their thoughts and feelings are the only instruments by which the All-Creative Energy can manifest in their lives.

It is of no avail to blame Providence, or other people, for your troubles.

No matter what form chaotic conditions take in your life you alone are responsible for them; and you alone can rectify them through use of your inseverable contact with God.

Once one learns through study and practice, or through experience, to allow the will of God (which is always good) to have free action in and through Him, then all bondage to conditions is over!

PUPIL: At the risk of appearing dull may I ask yet again just how this can be done by each of us?

MASTER: I have given you the answer a number of times in this book; but it is worth repeating in a little different form, for it is an ALL IMPORTANT item. Here is the answer yet again:

(1) Mentally go deep within your inmost self, your own Divine inmost, and ask yourself: "What DOES God really mean to me?" "What must the Divine Nature in me be like?"

(2) Once you have formed a definite and positive conclusion on these points, try to reproduce this same feeling all through your whole being. KEEP TRYING, and you will succeed in doing it. It is worth the effort required, a million times over.

(3) Do NOT let yourself be discouraged with this practice if you do not seem to get immediate results.

Remember always that Troward says "it is the intention that counts; it is the intention which registers on the reproductive disk of Creative Life."

(4) Another powerful help, to me personally at least, is to diligently use that affirmation from Troward which begins: "My mind is a center of Divine operation," etc. (See "Your Invisible Power," or Troward's "Dore Lectures"). The Lord's Prayer is also an excellent aid, as I have repeatedly written herein.

(5) Try, try, try with all of your concentrated purpose to live hourly in the feeling of the affirmation, or the prayer. Do not let yourself slip and fall by indulgence in what you may call "justifiable impatience" for there is no such thing. Anger, or jealousy, or fear, and all like things, will cause you to slip also, for these things are unlike your idea of God, or of God's thought.

PUPIL: That is a very tall order!

MASTER: Not when you realize constantly that it is the intention that counts. The more you keep your intention right the less frequently will you slip in your practice of these principles; and soon your whole life shall have been altered until it IS like your own conception of God.

PUPIL: Many people who seem to have a very good idea of Christian Science, Divine Science, Unity, etc., try very hard for more money, better health, higher social position. Yet they do not seem to get far. Why?

MASTER: Whether or not they are conscious of it they are looking to the outside as the source from which these things shall come to them. But the origin of all good things is within! All good is within your own lifestream; and this must be recognized!

Our recognition of the within, the spiritual, as the true source of all good things will give them form in the outer or physical, world in which we live.

Once the contact is made within, and faithfully held, the things will automatically come to pass in the outer. The whole secret is this:

We must know exactly who we are, what we are and why we are!

Knowing this, our contact with the source of all good is never interrupted. It is our task to take care of the inner things; and if we do, the outer things shall take care of themselves. then shall we go forward, and only forward, happily, harmoniously, serenely accomplishing any and all good things that we may wish!

Chapter 7

PERSONAL POINTERS ON SUCCESS

MASTER: No one ever slides into real success without personal effort. It takes all one has to attain unto real success, and to hold it: but by the very same law each person has all it takes! If we are willing to reach out for achievement, and to use all of our faculties to that end, then unqualified, constant success is surely ours.

It has been said that Napoleon never blundered into a victory.

He always won his battles IN HIS MIND before he won them on the field.

This is exactly what every successful person does!

PUPIL: What is the very first step on the high road to success?

MASTER: The very first step is to decide definitely and positively what form of success you want.

Henry Ford, for example, wished with all of his heart and soul to make better automobiles cheaper, cars that were within the financial reach of all persons.

Thomas A. Edison wanted to provide various efficient electrical appliances at moderate prices for the convenience and comfort of the world.

Jesus the Christ had one outstanding desire ever-present in His consciousness: To show the way for every human being to find the Father-Principle within himself, to show all how to find and know and trust that Infinite Divine Power which really will, and does, protect all, guide all, provide for all.

Each of these men had a divine urge that burned within him, an all-consuming passion to do one thing better than it may have been done before.

Because they knew exactly what they most wished to do they did it!

PUPIL: If one does not know exactly what line of endeavor to pursue, what is a good thing to look for in determining just what is best to do?

MASTER: Here is another most-important essential to success; this will give you your cue.

The more good a person can do for others with his product, his life, his work, or whatever it may be, the greater success will that person have!

No one ever succeeded in any very great degree whose dominant motive was that of personal gain only.

If one actually helps others, many others, to live happier, better, more successful lives, one need give little thought to the gain that will accompany the success; for if one does this the gain to self can not possibly be withheld. One's chief motive then in reaching out for success is not to see how much he may help himself but to see how greatly he may help many others.

PUPIL: These two steps are most helpful to me. But before taking other steps may I ask just what pitfalls I should look out for most when first I start on the road?

MASTER: Here are two of the most common snares, I think:

(1) Never yet has success come, and never shall it come, to any person who simply wishes for it. Mere wishes are idle and utterly impotent unless the wish is great enough to inspire one to immediate action. Yes, action, not wishes, is the big thing.

(2) Keeping your mind centered on the big success that you "are going to be" will never bring it to pass. You must know yourself successful now.

So long as one looks upon success as a future acquirement just so long will success be postponed, just so long will its attainment always remain future. From the very start one must learn to back up the thought with the feeling, the absolute conviction, that I AM success now!

PUPIL: These are splendid, too. Now I am ready for another step forward.

MASTER: Since you have now firmly resolved to make a business of acquiring true success in accordance with Life's immutable Laws, you must throw your whole energy into making your mind a center for positive thoughts only, for constructive thoughts only. You are deliberately careful of the words you use. You are deliberately careful of your mental reaction to the words you may hear.

For instance, if you hear people talking about a tornado you should not let your thoughts dwell upon destruction but rather upon tremendous power positively used. If you hear people talking about disease, you should inwardly know that while disease is a natural result of broken natural laws it is not necessarily evil, and that in Life as Life all is good and perfect.

In a word it will be necessary for you to avoid all detours, even though they may appear easy and short.

PUPIL: What are some of these detours? How will they be marked?

MASTER: All of them should be marked with lots of red lanterns for certainly they are dangerous to one seeking success.

Here are a few of them which you will recognize as questions that you have asked yourself, just as millions of other Truth-seekers; and yet they wonder why success always eludes them.

(1) "Well, why doesn't it come?"

(2) "when will it come?"

(3) "maybe this is the way it will come."

(4) "Perhaps it is not God's will that I have this."

Success does not come for the one who asks: "Well, why doesn't it come?" simply because he is asking why rather than knowing that it now is! For the one who whimpers: "When will it come?" it shall never come so long as he asks when.

What they wish now is or else it never will be.

And as concerns "God's will" for us His will for us is anything good we may desire.

PUPIL: Just why is it that if we wish success for ourselves only, for personal gain only, we shall not be apt to get it?

MASTER: Here is an illustration.

Suppose you went to your own personal banker and asked him for a loan of one hundred thousand dollars, knowing that he had that much, and more to loan and that your worth justified a loan of that amount.

No doubt his first question would be that one that bankers always ask first of anybody seeking a loan, i.e., "What do you want the money for?"

Let's suppose you answered: "Oh, I wish to take a year's cruise on my yacht, doing nothing, just loafing, resting, sleeping; eating. I need the change, you see."

Do you think he would let you have the money?

No not a soul!

No more will the Great Universal Banker (God) under like, or similar, circumstances. You must approach Him with a really good idea, one which will bring good to many, not just to yourself. I know men who have millions and who began with no money, who began only with an idea.

Their basic ideas were so universal towards the production of good they were able to secure from others all the money necessary to finance the beginning of their enterprises. The great secret of individual success is the very same as that of the national success that has made America the wealthiest land on earth, and is this:

Our men of affairs, of greatest success, have learned to share with all of our people through benefiting all of the people, either directly or indirectly, through dispensing higher quality goods at less cost, through sharing earnings more generously with employees, etc.

They have learned that it is an absolute science that giving to and sharing with many always have getting as a natural correlative! Get your thought right; capture an idea that will prove helpful to many; then draw in confidence on the Unlimited Banker for all that you require.

You will discover that you cannot keep money from gravitating to you. Herein lies sure and continuing success!

PUPIL: May we have here, in conclusion, the gist of this whole matter of true success, in summary form? This will facilitate ready reference by us who are students.

MASTER: Certainly you may have this. It may be said that the steps to success are seven in number; and here they are:

(1) Thoroughly make up your mind exactly what you want most right now.

(2) Be certain that your desire has in it the element of good for many. Then ask your own inmost soul for the most perfect idea, or ideas, relative to your desire, ideas that will produce good for many.

(3) Make a mental picture of your desire as fulfilled now, and now only, making the mental picture complete, vivid, alive with feeling. This is the meaning of Jesus' great statement to "ask believing that you (already) have." In the mental picture you actually do have (mentally, which is the realm of all true causation) your desire right now. Once you really get into the feeling that what you want already is yours (mentally) you will SOON realize how quickly it grows into actual form. Keep out of your mind all fear-habits of thought. Know that fear-habits can be readily changed into faith-habits. Fear and faith are the same, one being one end of the stick and the other the other end of the same stick. The fear end of the stick is a shovel and will surely dig the grave of success; the faith-end is a jeweled crown ready to adorn the head of any who will wear it.

(4) If necessary, compel yourself to implicitly believe that the same Power that give you your desire in the beginning will also give you the ways and means of its triumphant fulfillment.

(5) Meditate carefully at frequent intervals on the real purpose of your desire. This real purpose of the desire, or the thing, is the all-important spiritual prototype for the thing you want. Also go over the Lord's Prayer very carefully several times daily, it will help you much in meditating more profoundly, and will tune your mind in with the power (God).

(6) Every night before going to sleep, and every morning upon first awakening, make a solemn vow to live close to your God every conscious hour, to see only good in all, to entertain only good and constructive thoughts about everything and everyone.

(7) Frequently mentally see yourself already enjoying your fulfilled desire.

Do this every time you think of the desire; and especially at night and morning, just before sleeping and at once upon awakening, for at these periods the subconscious element of mind is especially amenable to suggestions.

In this way you do already have your desire perfectly fulfilled (mentally); and if you persist in it you shall surely have it soon in its physical form right in the midst of your life.

For example, the great bridge that now spans the Golden Gate at San Francisco was first pictured completed and in use by many in the mind of its designer before it became an actual reality.

But by mentally picturing the bridge as already completed and serving many people well the designer DREW from the whole universe the power necessary to have it actually built.

These seven points are the keys, or steps, to the attainment of real success in any line of endeavor, mark them well, and above all other things use them! They are Truth! They work!

Chapter 8

INSTANTANEOUS HEALING

MASTER: It seems strange to one who has made real progress along God's great highway of Truth just how many mortals who are on the same journey will make detours that are altogether unnecessary, or will even turn and go in the opposite direction from their desired goal.

For example, nearly everyone, it seems, is very much interested in a newly discovered disease, or in just disease as such, while the thing that all of us wish to know most about is perfect health and how to reach that rich experience that is spoken of in the Apocrypha, Ecc. 30:15-16, which reads: "Health and a good estate of body are above all gold: and a strong body above infinite wealth!"

Of course we all know that it is impossible to find the Truth about health by holding our interest and attention on disease.

PUPIL: But we know that there is disease. Must we not reckon with this fact?

MASTER: One who recognizes disease as a reality has thus made his own law about it, and for him disease is inevitable. If disease is what you think and believe then disease is a fact for you. All bodily inharmony is first a thought and a belief; consequently its CURE is from the mental side also. It has been said that "the Absolute (Spirit) is like the air which carries odors, both good and bad, but which remains forever untainted by them."

In the Absolute all is health and harmony; it may carry the beliefs of mortals in disease about with it yet it is never tainted by them!

PUPIL: But since the belief in disease is so widely prevalent is it not well for us to know how to handle disease, or belief in disease, from the spiritual standpoint?

MASTER: It would be more scientific to know how to handle health; and we shall devote this lesson to Healing, to living in conscious harmony with Life's laws. We shall start with the fine art of giving an effective spiritual treatment, or mental treatment.

There are a number of most important points for the healer, or practitioner, to always remember and always practice in this respect.

PUPIL: Which point is the most important of them all?

MASTER: That is difficult to answer since all of them are vitally important; but one of them is this:

- The practitioner should have firmly fixed in mind the fact that there is but one mind and but one expression of this one mind although it fills all space with its numberless manifestations.
- This awareness removes the line of demarcation between patient and healer.
- Another vital essential is this: If one hopes to be of any help to a patient one must not give treatment for disease. That would surely intensify the disease!
- In giving a spiritual treatment the practitioner should utterly dismiss all thoughts of disease and of personality from the mind.
- To hold the thought on disease would mean MORE disease.
- Rather the healer should mentally see Life whole, free, at peace and in harmony through the power of the Radiant Christ within.

PUPIL: But suppose the patient is right there in front of you at the time of the treatment, that he is ill and in great pain.

How can the practitioner avoid seeing the ill condition?

MASTER: If one is not sufficiently disciplined in mind to see through, or beyond, the condition one should not attempt to be a healer; or else such a one should confine his efforts exclusively to absent mental treatments.

To see, or to believe in, any condition that a patient may seem to have disarms a practitioner immediately and renders his efforts impotent in behalf of the patient.

PUPIL: Are the absent mental treatments always just as effective as ones given face to face? Does not the distance of the patient from the source of treatment raise a barrier to the effectiveness of the treatments?

MASTER: A well trained and experienced practitioner is able to treat just as effectively absently as presently; and there are some who do better work absently. In Spirit there is neither time nor space, and the distance of the patient from the healer makes no difference at all. you see the first mental step that the practitioner takes is that of clearing his or her mind of the presence of anything except the one god-spirit. Thought is unbelievably fast in its transmission and can span the earth instantly; and it does not lose any of its power in the transmission! In giving an absent treatment the healer should be positive that the thought sent forth reaches the recipient now and with infinite power.

PUPIL: Why is it so vitally important to know that the Truth for the patient is his now? If he is ill it does not seem quite reasonable to me that he could be made whole right now.

MASTER: Nevertheless it is either now or never! In the Absolute the ONLY time there is the eternal now. To it there is no past; nor is there any future. To it there is only the present. If the practitioner holds the thought that the patient "will be all right," it will always be "will be" for the patient because the healer is postponing the healing until some future time, and there is no future known to the Spirit, as I have said.

Did Jesus ever say to any of those who were healed by Him: "You will be healed. Arise and go"?

No, not ever.

Always He spoke to them in the present tense; always He told them something to this effect: "You ARE WHOLE! Go in Peace!"

PUPIL: Just what are the mechanics of giving a mental treatment for one who is present personally with the practitioner?

MASTER: The steps in giving a successful treatment under such circumstances are these:

(1) Have the patient RELAX physically as completely as possible, all over, toes, ankles, knees, spine, shoulders, arms, hands and even the eye-lids (for the eyes should be closed in the silence). The whole body of the patient should be as limp as possible. The greater the physical relaxation you may induce on the part of the patient the greater his RECEPTIVITY to the mental treatment will be.

(2) Have the patient "empty" his conscious mind as completely as is possible, trying to think of nothing at all insofar as this can be done; have him try to make a vacuum of his mind, as it were. This complete relaxation of the conscious mind also induces a much greater receptivity.

(3) The healer must completely remove the line of demarcation between the patient and self. There are not two persons present, not really, not patient and practitioner. The two are one, and the establishment of this fact firmly in the mind of the healer is of untold importance. Remember that Mrs. Jones, practitioner, is not giving Mrs. Smith, patient, a mental treatment. As long as the one treating is aware of any sense of separation, or distinction, between patient and self there will be little if any results achieved.

(4) Once all sense of separation is really removed from the practitioner's consciousness, the actual treatment is given. The patient is now in a passive, or receptive, attitude, both mentally and physically. The healer is in an active, or generating, position. Yet the "two" are one, the one person being the negative pole, the other the positive, and between them the healing current of Life may now freely pass. Into the Absolute the practitioner now projects a steady stream of positive, constructive, powerful thought-energy, at the beginning of which process the patient's name is either silently or audibly called in order that the flow of Spirit may be given definite direction.

The receptive attitude of the patient picks up the flow of power and so it is made his own. The affirmation the healer uses at the beginning of the silence may be said aloud once or twice although this is not necessary. Into the Bosom of the Spirit, into the Fruitful Silence, the practitioner thinks and dwells with intense concentration and feeling, yet without any sense of strain whatsoever.

PUPIL: Upon what thought does the healer dwell in the silence?

MASTER: Upon the spiritual prototype for the organ that may seem to be diseased, or for the thing or condition that may be desired. This spiritual prototype is yet another thing that is of vital importance. To dwell in thought upon anything physical, anything which has form, is to be on the plane of limitation, of secondary causation, of effect.

But to think steadily upon the spiritual prototype is to mentally be in the realm of the absolute which is the infinite, which is first cause or primary causation, which is the cause itself and not the effect.

PUPIL: To me this spiritual prototype, important though I am sure it is, is the hardest thing in all of this study "to get hold of" mentally, the most difficult point to really understand. May I have some helpful pointers on this matter?

MASTER: That is true of many, in fact for nearly all "beginners" in this study. Perhaps the spiritual prototype is difficult for you because it is FORMLESS,

Then, too, it may seem hard to understand because it is a new idea to you, one with which you are unfamiliar, of which you are not accustomed to thinking. Yet it is quite SIMPLE, once you know its nature.

Here are some good rules to follow in this matter:

(1) The spiritual prototype of anything is the thing itself in its most incipient state, is the actual origin of the thing in the Universal Mind.

(2) To find the spiritual prototype for anything it is only necessary to determine in your own mind the PURPOSE of the thing, whatever it may be. This is an infallible rule. Suppose, for example, one wished a good automobile and would like to know the spiritual prototype for it.

One would mentally ask: "Exactly what is the purpose of an automobile? What is it for? What does it do? What do I really want with a car" The automobile is, of course, an instrument, a means of progress, of rapid, pleasant, harmonious progress.

This being so, then the spiritual prototype for an automobile is progress. At least this is what a car means to me; but in selecting a spiritual prototype for anything each one should think out for himself just what the purpose of the thing is to you.

Chapter 9

INSTANTANEOUS HEALING (Cont'd)

PUPIL: Will you please give us a few other prototypes, and show us how they are arrived at? With still a few more examples to serve as guides, I am sure that I shall then know how to form my own prototypes for any particular thing desired or required.

MASTER: Very well; here are a few more. Let us take the head, for example, supposing that one had a belief in a violent headache.

The head is the house of the brain; and the brain is the instrument of the mind, but in no sense the mind itself. What is the purpose of the mind? It is to know, to know God, the capacity to know God!

Can a capacity to know ever really ache, or hurt, it being a formless thing? No it can not! The spiritual prototype for the head then, as I see it, is the capacity to know God.

Now for a minute let us consider the eyes. What is the purpose of the physical eye?

It is the instrument of discernment, which is a purely spiritual factor, discernment as such having no form of its own. The capacity of discernment is the spiritual prototype for the eyes, to me.

Here are a few other spiritual prototypes for you; and in these that now follow I shall not explain for you just how I arrived at the conclusion.

I shall name the particular organ, or part, of the body and the prototype for it, as I see it, and give you the benefit of thinking out for yourself just why I have chosen this particular prototype for each specific thing.

TEETH -Capacity to analyze and dissect God's ideas;

LUNGS -Capacity to know life as life;

HEART -Capacity of love;

STOMACH -Capacity of understanding;

LIVER -Capacity of faith;

KIDNEYS -Capacity of purity and cleanliness.

The spiritual prototype, please remember always, is the purpose of the thing.

Every physical thing has a purpose; consequently it has a spiritual correspondence.

By letting your thoughts dwell upon the purpose of any physical organ, or thing, you make direct and most powerful contact with the source of all things, with the first cause which projected forth from itself all concentrated things; for as Troward told me, "matter is only spirit slowed down to a point of visibility."

PUPIL: These examples will help me very much, I am sure. But now I am wondering just what is the best way to help ourselves, and others, forget human weaknesses, aches and pains, etc. It seems to me that most of us have the habit of dwelling too much in thought upon such negative things.

MASTER: I find that the very best way to get away from negative thoughts and feelings is this: to deliberately train the thought and feeling to travel along the road of our blessings!

Our every conscious moment DOES HAVE a blessing in it, if only one will look carefully for it, recognize it and be happy because of it. In looking for our blessings it will help greatly to recall to mind the many joys we have experienced, as well as those we hope to experience. In these ways we are able to forget the negative things of which the human side of us is so prone to accuse us.

PUPIL: May we have an illustration of this point, please? Something out of your own experience?

MASTER: Yes. Here is an actual experience in which I had a part. In Los Angeles several years ago a lady came to me with the problem of cancer, with which inharmony she had been told that she was grievously afflicted.

Her whole attention, it seemed to me, was rigidly held on the limitation the cancerous condition was causing her, or should soon cause her to know. She owned and operated a restaurant, and was doing much of the work herself. Several doctors, she said, had told her there was no cure for her, that the disease had spread until an operation was not to be considered, that she must stay off her feet and spend most of her time, such as remained to her, in bed, etc. This, she said, meant that she must go out of business, of course, and when she did that she would be in dire want, in fact an object of charity. With her mind filled with these negative thoughts of illness and lack, which were certain to come unless she could be healed, she came to see me.

When I had talked the matter over with her I asked her to let me think things over for three days before giving her my decision about accepting her case for mental treatment. I asked for this delay in order that I might thoroughly check to see how much time I could allot to her, to see if I could arrange for all the time she would require.

After two days of changing some appointments, and postponing some others which were not really urgent, I told the lady to come.

My first question to her was this:

"Do you absolutely believe what Jesus told His disciples, as recorded in Mark 10:27, and which reads as follows: 'With man it is impossible, but not with God; for with God all things are possible!"?

She assured me positively that she did believe just that; but said that she found her own mind too untrained and chaotic to keep her thought and feeling OFF what seemed to be the inevitable and hold it on the fact that God IS the only power there is, that he is forever present, always amenable to suggestion, eternally responsive and always creative. Hence she wished the help of the Spirit through me.

I told her that I should ask her to know with me HOURLY, continually, that her relation to God is always I-AM, and that whenever she thought or said "I-AM" to remember that she was thinking or saying, in reality, "GOD IS."

I told her also that God created her out of Himself, for Himself, and that to Him and in Him she was forever complete, whole, perfect. "God is love!"

I told her; and I asked her to always try to feel His Great Love surging through her. I quoted I John 4:16-18 to her: "God is love; and he that dwelleth in love dwelleth in god and god in him!"

I also asked her to know that God is life, Intelligent, Loving, Harmonious, Creative Life, and asked her to hold her conscious thought and feeling on these things.

"But," she protested, "you have not given me any affirmation for MY cancer!"

"Did you say 'MY cancer?" I asked her with much feeling and emphasis.

"Do you really want cancer, my dear? Are you determined to have it?

If not, then why are you claiming it for your own by saying 'MY cancer'? Remember thoughts are things!"

"Oh, no!" she exclaimed. "I see what you mean. Just listen to me. I must conquer this negative habit of thought."

I assured her yet again that she WAS a Divine Child, that all of her needs were forever supplied THROUGH HER RECOGNITION of them.

I then told her to try to constantly keep in her consciousness thoughts which contained some quality of the following:

Belief Confidence Conviction Credit Honesty Patience Reliance Sincerity and other ideas in which there was some of the essence of faith.

I stressed the fact that by keeping these things in mind her thought and feeling would have the essence of faith in them; and that she should soon form the HABIT of thinking in that way.

It was my endeavor to get her to keep her mind off herself and on the things of the spirit. I knew that if I could get her to do this habitually God should take care of the rest of the matter. This lady assured me that she would try to do exactly as I had asked although it seemed more plausible to doubt than to believe that she could be in perfect health again after so much suffering, and the opinions of several doctors that she was doomed.

Still again I told her most positively that it is written: "God is with you to save you!"

I asked her to remember that faith is alive and that it leads to more life which doubt is dead and leads nowhere. The leading characteristic of faith is that it constantly flows and burns with constantly increasing brightness and expectancy.

Faith always travels in the one direction of understanding. Doubt is a blight upon every effort towards Truth.

This patient came to see me regularly every day for some two weeks; and her condition began to improve from the very start. Then she had only absent treatment at frequent intervals, with an occasional visit in person, for another six weeks.

At the end of two months she was entirely free from any evidences of cancer, free in body, in mind and in affairs.

Immediately she began to build up physically and when I last saw her, some two of three years after she first came to me, she was in robust health, prospering in business and sure of her contact with the Spirit.

PUPIL: This illustration clears up in my mind, when I go back over it point by point, a number of ideas which were very hazy and uncertain to me. Thank you. I do know that doubts make one wretched from morning until night.

MASTER: Exactly so. And it would seem that after a while people who indulge in them would learn this fact and make an "about face" and a "forward march" in the direction of faith.

Faith is a brightly-glowing light and lives within us.

It has its source in the fountain-head of INTUITION. Its radiance is seen in the long shafts of splendor that lead one forever upward into the kingdom of the beautiful, the true, and the good.

PUPIL: If one does not have any faith, how does one get it?

MASTER: One does NOT get faith. Every soul already has it!

It has been yours forever; it is as much a part of you, of your Divine Being, as is your heart, your lungs, your mind: It is a gift as precious as Life itself, and is born of Life itself, forever innate in every living soul.

It is true that some are less aware of faith than others through having neglected it, through having blighted it with doubts, fears, anxiety, etc. But the quality IS still there, and by cultivation it will spring into fullness again. All that is required is this: that you exercise the faith that you already have for just a few weeks.

Deliberately look for it! Insist on seeing it! Persist in using it!

Chapter 10

IS DESIRE A DIVINE IMPULSE?

MASTER: Is desire a Divine Impulse? One hears this question asked in as many different forms, it seems, as there are humans.

So frequently is it propounded and discussed it seems to me that it will be helpful to answer it from Troward's standpoint; after you have studied and meditated upon it from his views you will arrive at your own satisfactory conclusion.

PUPIL: I am glad that you have brought this up for us. I have often wished I knew just what God wanted me to do when I have been undecided about some move, perhaps a momentous decision.

MASTER: The only way anyone can fully understand Life's law of attraction is through seeing what it does under certain given conditions.

In a tree it is growth; in an animal it is development; in all of nature it is evolution. From the lowest to the highest forms all growth is prompted by the organized creature pushing forth in its own accomplishment.

One can not do otherwise than believe in the law of unfoldment which is the hallowed desire of the All-Originating Life to see itself more and more fully manifested. Since we as humans are branches of the one and only tree of Life this fact is also true of us.

PUPIL: May I ask a question, please?

MASTER: Certainly, any time.

PUPIL: Do you mean that all growth is a result of a desire for self-expression, that all evolution is within the great Creative Mind?

MASTER: Just so; and each of us is a direct result of that desire.

Therefore we should learn to trust our desires! There is but the ONE great desire and practically all of our individual desires are reflections of that one.

Man's desire, his real desire, is for good.

No rational person would desire anything else for himself or another.

PUPIL: But many philosophies teach that we must conquer, must overcome, must rise above all desire in order to be perfected. How do you answer this?

MASTER: I stand fast in what has already been said herein. I hold fast to the firm conviction that our desires are divine impulses which stimulate us to growth and constant development. Without desires we should be mere automatons, should have no wish to progress and grow.

It is impossible for one to crush out all desires without Ruining self, spirituality, physically, morally and mentally. The desires, the longings, we have are stimuli, are urges for expression, from the holy citadel of God within ourselves!

PUPIL: Is it true then that if we would draw into us any particular benefit we have only to impress the desire for it firmly upon the subconscious phase of mind and hold it unwaveringly? Should we do this just as an impression of sound is made upon a phonograph disk before being reproduced? Should we do this knowing that said desire is instantly transmitted into the One Great Creative Energy which is always responsive, and that is sure to be manifested in our own physical world?

MASTER: That is just what I mean. Let me give you another illustration.

I know a very fine and very wise lady in Los Angles who after returning from marketing found that she had misplaced her car keys; and she had an urgent appointment awaiting her downtown within a little while. She had taken her groceries from the car into the kitchen. After looking around for the keys in every place that she could logically think of she had still failed to find them.

So she told herself (her subconscious phase of mind); "I want those car keys. I must have them. Now where are they?

You know!"

Almost immediately she had the desire to empty the bag of potatoes into the kitchen sink. But she ridiculed that idea, and repeated her desire to find the keys. She did this two or three times, meanwhile keeping up her search for the keys; and every time she received back the feeling that she should empty the potato-bag.

It was her habit to let her maid empty the bags and put the purchases away; and the idea of emptying the potato-bag seemed foolish anyway. But the impulse remained urgently with her although she could not see how her car keys could possibly be in the potato-bag.

So she did empty the bag into the sink and almost instantly she heard a metallic sound.

She looked and, behold, there were the missing keys!

PUPIL: Her deep desire to find the keys brought her the answer? It seems very simple.

MASTER: And it IS very simple once you know the responsiveness of the law of subjective mind. This lady knew that law.

PUPIL: If she really knew the law why did she not recognize the answer to her desires the very first time she was impressed to empty the potato-bag?

MASTER: The lady to whom I refer is a very highly-educated woman, a keen student of logic. While she truly does believe in the intuitive power of the mind to capture an idea from the Infinite the old race-habit of giving reason first place had not been entirely uprooted from her consciousness.

When intuition told her plainly to empty the bag reason set up an argument and told her that the impulse was foolish.

The controversy between reason and intuition continued within her for several minutes. Then because of her study of Truth, and her application of it, she was reminded that intuition, and not logic, is the true key of life! So she was impelled to do as she was bidden.

When she did so her desire had fulfillment as its correlative. Always desire and fulfillment are bound together as cause and effect through the universal law of attraction!

PUPIL: It still seems to me that a true student of Truth should have thoughts, feelings and desires so trained in the right direction that logic could not go wrong in its conclusions.

MASTER: One does not change life-long habits of reasoning overnight. Like everything else, complete change is a matter of growth.

The fact that she did obey the still small voice within, and that thus was her problem solved, are all that really mattered.

In time this lady, like all of us, will learn to instantly recognize the voice of intuition when it speaks and will no longer question, nor reason, will only obey.

When we all reach that point, as we can and shall through faithful study and practice, there will be no problem in all of human experience that will fail to yield its answer! There is a lot of truth in the old saying: "Take care of the heart and the head will take care of itself."

PUPIL: But is not the road to the attainment of true wisdom a long, hard one?

MASTER: It is long alright, being Infinite in scope; but it is NOT hard. It is like the story of the two men who are walking to Rome. One asked the other why he had chosen a road that was so full of stones. His companion replied that he had not been aware of any stones in the road, and suggested that they sit down by the roadside and take off their shoes.

This they did; and the one who had been complaining found a PEBBLE IN HIS SHOE. But there was nothing wrong with the road itself.

PUPIL: The road is then what each one makes of it for himself? Is that your idea?

MASTER: That is right. The broad highway of Truth is in fact, to me at least, the most interesting road in all of life. It takes times and interesting, happy effort to establish an unbroken consciousness of the perfect reciprocal action between the desire for expression as it exists in the Creative Energy and in the individual mind. It is true that by rightly establishing our relation to the Great Parent Mind we can gradually grow into any condition that we may desire, provided of course that we first make of ourselves, through our habitual mental attitude, the person who corresponds to those conditions.

One can never get away from the Law of Correspondences.

This science of Correspondence, or of cause and effect, is as infallible as is mathematics; and as in mathematics its principles must be mastered before one can habitual feel: "My Father and I are ONE!" Yes, our desires are our own immortal selves seeking fuller expression; and one may soon prove to the doubting, bewildered self that one.

PUPIL: Somehow it is still a little difficult for me to accept the feeling that my desires are Divine impulses, or the Divine Nature Itself seeking expression through me. It seems to me that desire is selfish and often wrong, even bad for one.

MASTER: Did not Jesus say; "Seek and ye shall find!" Just why would anybody seek a thing?

PUPIL: Because he wanted that for which he was seeking.

MASTER: Very good. Are not wants and desires the same? Jesus also said: "ASK believing that you have and ye shall have!" Why would one ask for a thing?

PUPIL: Because he desires it and feels it would be good for him.

MASTER: Correct. Yet again the Master said: "Except ye become as a little child ye shall in no wise enter the kingdom of heaven." If one desires to grow into the new life of liberty and joy, indeed one must become as a little child.

PUPIL: And just what did Jesus mean by that?

MASTER: Just what He said. Observe a child, any child, rich or poor. Its very impulse is desire, is to want something. All children are simply one continual incarnation of "gimme" and "want to." Naturally the child's wants are but the forerunner of the man and his wants; and in the adult desires are as natural as in the child.

PUPIL: This desire idea is truly a new one to me. But I like it.

MASTER: You will learn to love and trust your desires as your spiritual understanding expands. Vitality, which is Life, is born of desire, is the child of Love. You will be amazed at the rapid progress you will make once you have really made up your own mind to trust your desires. The more you learn to trust your wants the greater will be your flow of faith.

PUPIL: But must there not be a check somewhere on desires? A sorting of the good and the bad? All desires are not holy, are they?

MASTER: One must be rational, of course. Troward writes in his "Edinburgh Lectures" that "there is nothing wrong with the evidences of a healthy mind in a healthy body." This study presupposes that a sincere student of Truth will not harbor evil desires, that his or her mentality is normal, the behavior normal. This being so the desires of such a one should also be only natural, rational, good; and if this is so then the desires of that one are Divine impulses. Let me suggest that you read the personal letter that Troward wrote to me, an exact copy of which is found in my book, "Attaining Your Desires". Then you will see yet more clearly why you should trust your desires, recognizing as you do that desires are divine impulses!

Chapter 11

SUPREME SELF-FREEDOM

PUPIL: So, supreme self-freedom is our very wonderful subject for today, is it? I am sure that you shall prove to us that supreme self-freedom can be ours, that mind does rule the world.

MASTER: You may always be quite certain that your mind rules your world; and you may always know that your individual world is a branch of the Universal World. Your mind makes of your world a thing of beauty, peace and absolute freedom, if only you so will.

PUPIL: I am convinced that this is true IF only one could truly control one's mind, thoughts and feelings at all times. I know that others have attained this mastery, this self control; but somehow it does not seem to be for me, as much as I desire it.

MASTER: At one time in our lives each of us thought this same thing about the multiplication-tables. How difficult they seemed to us as children; yet each of us mastered them by persistent effort. It is like that with absolute self-freedom. It is dormant within each soul, waiting only for us to call upon it, to arouse it, to recognize it, to give it our attention, our concentrated observation, in our every thought, our every feeling, every act. It is not difficult to have if we make it first in our lives just as a great scientist puts his science before everything else! In theory at least all of us realize that we get only what we reach for and reach for steadily.

PUPIL: Is not Annette Kellerman, the great swimmer, an example of this? Was she not a cripple as a child, and considered hopelessly crippled?

MASTER: Yes, she was. But through insistent, persistent, determined, steady effort she became the physically-perfect woman, a model for the women of the world. Her science was the science of health, the science of physical beauty and perfection. There are many sciences; and each of us may select the one with which we are most in tune and pursue it to a dazzling goal.

PUPIL: But has not science boasted that it has Disproved the Holy Bible?

MASTER: It may be that some scientists make this boast.

But it is not true.

The fact of the matter is that science has confirmed the truth of the bible! It might be said that science has written a new Bible for the thinking mind merely by clarifying the old one. Science has made of the Bible, the Book supreme for those who are determined to live here and NOW. Science has proved

that "the word" of Life, of the Spirit, is a living word of power!

Truly "the heavens do declare the glory of God, and the firmament sheweth His handiwork."

In reading your Bible always substitute the word "Subconscious Mind" for the word "Lord." Try this faithfully for awhile and see what an astonishing growth you will make.

Try this with such passages as Isaiah 40:31, Mark 29:30, Luke 18:29-30 and a host of others.

Look about you; look at the results achieved by those who have learned to LOVE, to USE and to TRUST the MIND.

Strength, power, beauty, television, wire photography, microscope, telescope, spectroscope, all of these, yes ALL of ALL THINGS, are RESULTS from the Great Creative Energy whose progress, harmony; telephone, wireless, airplanes, chief attributes are these:

1. It is ever-present, everywhere;

2. It is always amenable to suggestion;

3. It is forever responsive;

4. It is eternally creative.

This God-energy, remember, manifests in the mind of man, in fact IS the mind of man.

The three Bible-references given above, and many others, teach us that if one puts the development of the divine spark within first, over all else, the divine in return will make that one first with it! Truly then the best Life has to give is the possession of that one!

PUPIL: Am I right in believing that the precious promises of the Bible all hinge upon our making intelligent decisions, Loving Life (God) first in everything? And if I do is everything I may desire sure to be mine?

MASTER: That is right, if you make god first, if you really do make him first. that is to say we should make it our first effort to know life's laws and to live them!

In this connection please read over and over again, or better still memorize letter perfect, the 22nd Chapter of Job,

beginning at verse 21 and continuing to the end of the Chapter. The promises given there, the power, the freedom, the

plenty, ARE yours, exactly as promised, if you will take the time, the effort, to become acquainted with the loving parentpower which is always able, and ever more than willing to do these things in you, through you.

As you read be sure to bear in mind constantly that the 21st verse is the key to all of the others that follow it.

The gist of this whole passage in job is this: we get out of life exactly what we put into it, plus much increase as interest

on our faith!

Some state this in a more homely way by saying that "we get what we pay for, and no more."

PUPIL: I have often wondered about this in connection with tithing. Is it true that tithing is a very old Law which has the greatest power back of it?

MASTER: Indeed tithing is a law which has much power in it!

I have tithed for twenty-five years, religiously so.

The practice of tithing is a divine-habit-forming virtue.

People tithe because they recognize God and wish to develop their recognition and expectancy.

Regular, systematic tithers are those who have formed the habit of counting their blessings. As a result their blessings constantly increase!

Did not Abraham give a tenth of his all to Melchizedek as a token of acknowledgment that his successes were from God? And when Jesus sent His disciples forth into the cities of Israel He expressly forbade them to take with them any money or provisions. Why? Because He wished the people of those cities to recognize God in His servants, and to support them with their tithes. As Saint Paul said: "The people who receive spiritual instruction shall administer some of their good to him who gives the instruction." It is a fact abundantly proved that the habit of tithing is a sure road to supreme self-freedom!

PUPIL: Am I to understand that the habit of tithing would give me a consciousness of an abiding partnership with God? Because my tithing is to God and His servants? Is this correct? Does one tithe to God's cause in recognition, in loving recognition, of Divine guidance? Does one necessarily have to tithe to churches only?

MASTER: No, one need not tithe to churches only.

Some people tithe regularly to missionary organizations, some to charities, and many tithe to individuals who work in God's vineyards, irrespective of organizations or affiliations.

The value of tithing lies in the establishment of the feeling of constant divine partnership.

Tithing brings one into the high and fruitful consciousness of God and company, unlimited!

If one keeps in CONSCIOUS touch with the Ever-Present, Responsive Substance of Life by regularly returning to it some of the substance (funds) which it has placed in his stewardship, this constitutes a practical acknowledgment of blessings and thus increases the blessings manifold.

The ancient Israelites proved this fact consistently; and for centuries the Jews have practiced tithing, as they do today.

The Mormons of today prove this Law constantly also. When I was lecturing in Salt Lake City during the "Depression"

there was not a single Mormon, or Mormon family on relief! The reason is obvious. They tithe!

PUPIL: I did not realize that tithing was so very great a stimulant for the steady inflow of supply; but now it seems to me that it would give one the same sense of security one has when the taxes are paid in full.

MASTER: That is right.

After all your money is yourself; You are God's, your money is His also.

Humanity exchanges its abilities, integrity, labor, etc., for money. In my thirty-five years as a practitioner I have had thousands of people come to me for spiritual help for increased supply; BUT in all of that time I have never had a solitary tither seek my help for financial increase!

In fact I have had very few tithers, ones who religiously follow the practice, ever seek my help for any kind of inharmony!

Tithing does carry with it a wealth of blessings.

Giving is worship!

If one really worships God, and considers Him one's best business partner, one acknowledges His help by giving to His cause first.

The average person gives a mere pittance to God, After they have paid everything else.

That is not tithing in any sense. A tithe is not a tithe unless it is ten percent.

The tithe should be paid first, from the gross profit; and it should be tendered in genuine love, thanksgiving and joy, if not in sheer abandon.

PUPIL: Is tithing required by the Intelligent, Creative Power in Life? Surely God does not need the money, or lands, or cattle.

MASTER: Tithing is voluntary.

Yet it IS required if one wishes a continual increase of blessings. It is a great joy to recognize God as a partner. To me a partner means one of whom we are fond, with whom we labor for a common good, and with whom we happily share in love. In order to receive benefits from tithing there must be joy in giving. To tithe grudgingly yields no blessings, or few at best. "He who gives himself with his gifts feeds three, himself, his hungering neighbor and me!" Tithing brings with it an abiding sense of security, has within its loving bosom an abundance of success-ideas which when adopted bring health, wealth and happiness.

This is the law of tithing.

PUPIL: Thank you for this lesson on tithing. I should like to hear much more about it. But are you going to tell us today how to reason ourselves into certainty?

MASTER: This is hardly what I meant when we were discussing reasoning out an affirmation before trying to absorb it.

For example let us consider freedom.

Freedom is joy; joy is freedom. But it seems there are few who have either freedom or joy to any great extent. Many seem to be bound by miseries; their every day is full of discord. To them work, all kinds of work, is disagreeable. To them most people are unbearable; things that happen are awful. The weather is abominable; it rains when it shouldn't; when it should rain it doesn't. They buy things, then regret it. They sell things and then are hurt because they didn't receive more money. If they don't go places they feel slighted; if they do go places they feel sure they were snubbed. If they don't have things they are despondent; if they do have things they are not what they want, etc., etc., etc.

PUPIL: Heavens, is this the average person you are describing?

MASTER: No. I am just giving you an intimate glimpse of a person in bondage, of ones who have not trained their minds to hold only thoughts of absolute freedom. Perfect joy and freedom are yours NOW. take them and make them yours.

PUPIL: How may one enter upon these joy thoughts at will?

MASTER: That is the place for the affirmation. Take, for example, the thought: "the very best life has to give is mine

now!" Reason about this for a minute. Why is it true? Because Life (God) made me out of Himself and LIVES IN ME. The very life of me is God. Life is happy; life is free; life is health; life is wealth; Life is all good.

PUPIL: I can see this BUT suppose that when you have satisfied yourself this is true some member of the family, or some friend, jabs you with a very unkind remark? What then? Are you supposed to laugh that off?

MASTER: If you really are conscious that the best Life has to give is yours, you will instantly realize at all times that you are not supposed to try to live for another. You have all you can do to keep the stream of joy flowing through your own consciousness.

When I first began my study with Troward he cautioned me every day:

"Watch your thoughts and feelings! They do take form, you know!"

And he really got that great Truth across to my consciousness.

When I went to Ruan Manor to study with him, I had been accustomed to a personal maid all of my life. I took my maid with me when I went to Troward. There was not one modern convenience where I lived in Ruan Manor; and none could be obtained thereabouts. We had been there just a month when Marie came to me in tears and told me she was heartbroken to leave me but she could not stay in that awful place any longer; she just must go back to Paris. She was too lonely, etc. Of course my first thoughts were: "If Marie goes, what shall I do? Here we are miles from anywhere, with no conveniences of any kind. What does this mean? Why should this disaster come to me now, of all times, when I really am trying to know God?"

Just when my thoughts reached that station, and were gathering momentum, Troward's warning: "watch your thoughts!" came to my mind and I stopped right there.

I began to use the will exercise he had taught me. I also used affirmations he had given me, to hold my thoughts where the Creative Power in thoughts and feelings could produce what I wanted. What I wanted most was freedom to continue with my study. I deliberately held my thoughts in the right place.

Only two days later the lady from whom I rented our rooms came to me and said she believed that Marie had been trying to tell her that she was leaving me (Marie was French and spoke no English) and that she wished she could find me another good personal maid before she went to Paris. I told the lady this was the case. She said that her daughter was coming home from London in just a few days, that her daughter had worked there for several years as a good personal maid, and that she felt sure the girl would be happy to work for me in that capacity. Marie left after teaching the other girl just how I wished things done; and the new maid was as satisfactory as the first. In this episode I had my first good lesson in knowing that I must watch my thoughts, that they do become things!

PUPIL: You have said that your favorite affirmation is the Lord's Prayer. Please show us how you would reason this out in order to better understand it before using it, part of it at least.

MASTER: Very well. The first two words of that prayer carry a tremendous power, if they are thought over, or spoken, with much feeling.

What does "Our Father" suggest?

Our Father, our very own Father?

When you were a child what was your idea of your father?

Your idea of him may have been exaggerated but you believed him to be rich beyond all words, influential, kind, loving, good, always ready to give, to help, to comfort, to make you happy and to see that you had everything that your little heart could desire. Then try to feel yourself as a child of God, with all the enthusiasm of a child. Know that you are so

like Him that He adores you, guides you, shields you, protects you, gives you everything He has to give in generous quantity, that you are, and that you have, His all.

Do this with the whole prayer.

Think about it all, understand and assimilate it all; then use it all!

If you will do your part you will find that the Father-Principle in life is always responsive! Your objective quality of mind may not know what is best for you because it can only realize the objective and limited side of Life. But the Father in you, he knows! Ask Him, be guided by Him. Your real desires are but reflections from Him which shine through and register in your mind.

PUPIL: Would it not be a good idea for us to frequently refer back to the lesson on "Desire, a Divine Impulse" when there is any confusion of mind about desires?

MASTER: Yes, that is recommended; in fact I trust that you will frequently review all of the Lessons of this Course. And I devoutly wish that you would earnestly try to make god first in your heart, and mind, and soul, and daily and hourly life.

If you will, it will mean for you a life of supreme self-freedom and truly you will make of yourself a reflection of God's own idea who is the perfected you. To this end I recommend the following, all of which I urge you to memorize, letter perfect. I also URGE you to use and use and yet again use these points and affirmations, faithfully and regularly. Here they are: For daily, Systematic, Loving Use: Your hourly effort should be that of fully realizing your true place in the Great Plan of Life. Just what is this true place for each individual?

It is, as Troward taught me, the following three things:

1. worship of God Alone;

2. The absolute equality of all individuals;

3. Complete control of all else.

Affirmations:

1. I AM intelligent, Loving Spirit, living in Creative Love and Power! In Him do i live and move and have my whole being!

2. I AM a specialized part of God's own Self-Manifestation! God IS specialized in me; therefore I AM perfect Harmony!

3. I AM direct knowledge of All Truth! I AM perfect Intuition! I AM Spiritual perception at its fullness! There is but One Wisdom; therefore I AM Perfect Wisdom!

4. My mind is a center of divine operation; therefore I AM always thinking good thoughts, speaking only constructive words! Time is Eternal; God is the only Giver! His Loving Intelligence is continually working in and through me; hence I AM ever working correctly. I AM thinking the right thoughts, in the right way, at the right time, towards the right result! God's work in and through me is always well done!

5. I AM Specialized Spirit! I AM always receiving rich, powerful inspirations from the Great, Universal, Parent Spirit. Divine Intelligence is always thinking new, fresh, clear ideas through me, ones far beyond any I have ever known before. My prayers are the outflow of the Great Oversoul of the Universe. They go forth in His Name; and always they accomplish that for which I send them. God is glorifying himself in and through me now!

Chapter 12

EXERCISES FOR HEALTH

1. Breathing, Bathing and Short, Easy, Profitable Exercises for Health:

Note: (These exercises are given as a stimulant to your capacity, both mental and physical. Mind and body are one. When both body and mind are strong happiness and success usually follow, especially if one adds to them mental and bodily efficiency.)

Correct breathing is one of Nature's most powerful methods of building a powerful body, a perfect body. Let us begin now to breathe correctly and profitably. If these exercises are taken as intended there will not be any strain.

The first exercise is this:

Upon arising in the morning first drink two or three glasses of water. The effect will be better if you will take the water just as hot as you can bear to drink it, with the juice of one-half a lemon in it.

Then stand erect, or else lie flat on the floor.

Exhale completely. Whether standing or lying on floor bend knees slightly.

As you exhale contract both the chest and the diaphragm, pushing the latter OUT and DOWN as far as possible without causing strain. Naturally this will extend the abdomen.

Then without lifting your chest pull abdomen IN as far as you can.

Then without any attempt at correct breathing push abdomen OUT and IN rapidly at least twelve times.

After you have mastered the above exercise for the abdomen and diaphragm, take the next exercise -for not more than two minutes each time.

This exercise is:

Stand erect, or lie flat on the back.

Exhale completely, contracting chest.

Then slowly inhale through the nostrils, trying not to allow chest to move.

Let the diaphragm push the abdomen down, then hold the breath for three or four seconds. Exhale slowly.

Then forget all about abdomen and diaphragm and inhale deeply, letting breath lift chest walls up and out to their fullest capacity.

Hold breath a few seconds and exhale all the breath.

If you will practice these two simple exercises each morning for ten days, you will note a great improvement in physical condition and vitality, the head and mind will be clearer and you will have a real zest for work.

No doubt you know that the right kind of bath is a splendid nerve-tonic, as well as a most important point in attaining physical and mental perfection.

When bathing for cleanliness the water should be of blood temperature, never hot or cold.

After the cleansing bath, fill the washbasin with cold water.

Scoop up two handfuls and apply to the forehead, and rub up and down the face.

Dip hands in cold water again and shake off all surplus water, then rub off balance behind the ears.

Repeat process on back of neck.

These things soothe and strengthen the nerves.

A certain way of relief for constipation is this:

First, meditate on the perfect and harmonious action of Life.

In Nature one does not find either inaction or over-action. Think over how the Life in your body regulates the flow of blood, the action of the muscles, both voluntary and involuntary, and how all of these things are done in perfect harmony.

For a regulatory exercise in relieving constipation the following is splendid.

First, as soon as you arise in the morning, drink two glasses of hot water.

Then stand, or lie on the back on floor.

Breathe deeply. As you inhale extend the abdomen and contract it as you exhale, contracting it all you possibly can. Do this without letting chest rise at all.

Do the exercise rapidly, vigorously, always inhaling through the nostrils and exhaling through the mouth.

Take about eight seconds for each complete breath.

Do this for a minute or two then use another minute to recover normal breathing.

A second exercise is recommended; and it is better if taken in connection with the one just given.

It is this:

Again stand erect or lie on the back, preferably the latter.

Draw first the right knee and then the left up to the chest as snug as possible.

Inhale deeply as you put foot down to floor and exhale as you draw knee down to chest.

Do this exercise rapidly, vigorously for one minute.

After the exercise try to get into the feeling of gratitude that you are able to consciously tune in with the harmonious action of Life. If you keep thinking deeply on the fact that all of the qualities of life must be present anywhere and everywhere that life is, the feeling of one-ness will come and you will enjoy the thrill of it.

The very best there is is yours now and the perfect movement is manifesting now.

3. How to Retain Youth and to Banish Gray Hairs and Wrinkles if They Offend You:

Think, know, feel, be thankful for the fact that Life as Life has NO age and yet is ageless.

Give this fact a little profound thought every day. Soon you will get the deep and abiding awareness of it. In your mind's eye, and in memory, try to recall how you felt about certain things when you were twenty, how you looked then, and acted, and bubbled over with energy. Ask yourself if your point of view about Life in general has changed radically, or if you have simply forgotten how to Live Life and Love it, as you did then.

The emotions, the fine understanding, the zest for activity, as you had them in youth have not glided off without leaving a trace in the development of your advancing years. Try to give yourself a careful going over mentally each day, and live for a while each day the experiences of your youth, bringing them back into your feeling. Perhaps you say: "Oh, but youth is so foolish!" That may be so; but remember always that it does things!

Try to weed out and destroy the doubts of your advancing years; try to prune out of yourself, out of your thought and feeling, your tendency towards being overconservative. Old age is only an ossified idea! Being over-conservative and opposed to progress and change are the things that make one old, and usually impotent. Your youth was all right; Live it again! Live it in Feeling and keep the feeling bolstered temporarily by making mental pictures of your happy, cocksure self as you were at twenty. See your face, figure and hair as they were then. And each day do the following exercise for the banishment of gray hair.

Vigorously RUB the whole scalp, from the nape of the neck up over the crown to the hair-line on the forehead, using Glover's Mange Cure. This liquid is not for dogs only, but is also an excellent tonic and stimulant for human hair. Rub the liquid well into the scalp. The gray hair may fall out for a while after you have done this exercise faithfully for several days but keep it up and new hair will come in with the natural color of the hair of your youth.

Yes, mentally go back to twenty and balance its vitality with your present wisdom!

KNOW with all of your heart and soul, and all of your emotional self, that Life as Life IS manifesting in you in a particular way in order that it may find new avenues for expressing itself as the JOY of living.

Make an hourly effort to keep in your consciousness your joys only. Make them register! Deliberately be happy and your body will respond to it in every way. It will also help, particularly for the ladies, to sit in front of the vanity a halfhour each day, seeing yourself not as you are now (if aged) but as you were in youth.

Do this with deep concentration, deepest feeling, affirming something like this:

"I AM Life. I AM youth, eternal youth!"

The important thing, however, is to see yourself as youth, to feel youth, to know that you are youth. Soon you will find a decided improvement setting in. Thought IS always creative! Soon you will look younger; soon you will feel younger; soon you will be younger, not in years of course but years do not make aging. Some are old at twenty-five; others are young at eighty.

It is flexibility of mind, a keen enjoyment of living, that make for elasticity of muscle and for youth.

4. A Method of Attracting Money:

Meditate on the riches of Life as it really is.

All that we can see or think of in Nature shows us only abundance. Every growing thing is amply provided for. The grass and trees, and other growing things, do not know poverty. In the soil, in the air, in the sunshine, there is an abundance of nourishment for all. Think about this great fundamental Truth because it applies to you also.

Wherever you may be, whatever your station in life may be, the Creator of all Life has just as amply provided for you as He has for the grass, the birds, all of Nature. It is not His fault that all do not express or manifest this bounty; people are as poor, or will soon be as rich, as they accept for themselves in the consciousness.

Everything that your individual nature may require has already been provided for you by the Creator. One has only to accept it, first in consciousness then in fact. Your steady recognition of this fact forms a veritable magnet in the mind which will attract every requirement to you, not as money that will drop in your lap without effort but as ideas, which when acted upon, will yield an abundant harvest.

Try this.

Begin right now to take the time, two or three times daily, to focus your thought at the base of the brain:

"Spirit of God (Life), I AM grateful to you for the abundance that is mine now!"

Any other good affirmation that may appeal to you, one that you compose for yourself perhaps, will do provided the use of it lifts your thought and feeling into certainty that abundance IS yours now. The more completely you can flood your mind, your consciousness, with the recognition of Life's abundance, for you as well as for all, the more quickly your thought and feeling will manifest in form. rich ideas will come to you intuitively, particularly if you impress the riches that are yours now upon your mind just before going to sleep. Any good idea if acted upon with wisdom and energy will yield great abundance for any one who apprehends it and works in faith towards its fulfillment.

5. The Value of Sleep and a New Method of Inducing It:

Sleep is Nature's restorative for tired tissues and often is found to be the only effective refreshener of the body machine.

The exact amount of sleep required varies with different individuals, much depending upon how fatigued a person is when retiring.

If one feels the need of relaxation and sleep, and yet cannot easily go to sleep, try the following method, which you may have read in my book, "The Healing Power is Life."

It is this:

Sit nude on the edge of your bathtub, feet outside the tub.

Take a fountain syringe and fill it with water that is blood-warm (NOT hot).

Place the end of the tube at nape of neck and let the warm water trickle down your spine until you begin to feel relaxed;

Then go to bed quickly, comfortable, warm and relaxed.

Another aid towards relaxation (and relaxation, if complete, is sure to induce sleep in a weary person) is this:

Lying in bed, on the back,

Deliberately send the message down to your toes, firmly, "Relax!"

Continue sending the message until the toes do spread and relax.

Then relax ankles in same manner, also knees, then base of spine, and the spine itself to base of head, also hands and arms.

As a rule one will never get this far with the relaxation-exercise; almost invariably one will slip off into deep, restful sleep before having consciously relaxed more than half the body.

Upon awakening if you feel recuperated, don't force yourself to remain in bed, whatever the hour.

Get up and do something that you are interested in doing.

Be sure the room you sleep in is always well ventilated; almost all people breathe more deeply when sleeping than when awake, unless exercising quite freely.

Do not eat a big meal just before retiring.

If you will give this method of inducing sleep a fair trial, you will find it very effective in inducing refreshing sleep that will have a real recuperative value.

Chapter 13

"HOW TO LIVE LIFE AND LOVE IT!"

MASTER: If you are anxious and uncertain about the future because of the fast-moving and extremely chaotic changes now going on all about you, here is a lesson that will help you find your true self and to stay at peace. Once we really find the true self we are in tune with Life as it is. Then we can live life and love it! Life really is glorious once one knows how to live it. Try to imagine for a few minutes that you know a secret which opens all of the closed doors of seeming limitation and that you can then step into a new world in which all is Life and Liberty. In order to enter this fair paradise of freedom the mind must be trained to choose carefully the emotional trend of thinking.

PUPIL: Do you mean that only those who have developed their different mental faculties through study and practice of Truth can enter this kingdom?

MASTER: That is exactly what I mean, since thoughts alone are creative. Those who have leaned the value of the trained will, imagination, intuition, and who live accordingly, can really feel secure. The tendency of thought, the habits of thought, determine with precision one's outward affairs. So as you start to travel this road which leads to absolute liberty in all things it is necessary to leave behind all excess baggage such as self pity, intolerance, criticism, fear, despondency, feelings of superiority, and all other negative and destructive occupants of your mental house. Take all these and put them in a secure bag; then tie a string of resolute determination tightly around them and dump them on a trash-pile. Cover the worthless bag of destructive evils with oil and set it on fire. Then are you really ready to start on your journey.

PUPIL: It would seem that one is only able to "go places" on this road by developing self-control. Is that so necessary?

MASTER: Yes, vitally necessary. However true and powerful a truth may be there must be a method of application of the principle to the individual. The best and surest method of manifesting the truth that God and man are one, and that God lives in and thinks through each of us, is to deliberately cultivate self-control with its consequent serenity of mind. In your endeavor to use this great Power for your individual purpose in the affairs of your hourly life you must be able to catch your thought the minute it begins to wander into doubts, fears, condemnations, criticisms, etc. and turn it in the direction you DO wish to go. Thus will you build certainty into your soul and body and the possession of certainty within means certainty and all things good in the affairs.

PUPIL: You make it seem that my disposition and self-control need much of my attention. I will admit that I am not patient; and of course I am intolerant, but only with those who deserve it -only with those who do not seem to try to do their part do I lose my temper.

MASTER: It is not my intention to be personal about your disposition. But I do say earnestly that every person who wishes to enjoy the blessings of true freedom must learn careful thought-selection, which means absolute thoughtcontrol, or self-control. In this way you will very soon entertain only the thought-guests you admire and enjoy. The uncouth, the grouchy, the selfish, the condemnatory, the suspicious, the tramp thoughts, all of whom will try to make a convenience of your mental domain, must be turned out of your mind. The best way to do this is put your whole feeling into an affirmation, whatever one appeals to you at the moment. Hold steadily to that thought and feeling until everything unlike it is out of your mind. Then lock your mental doors and use your will to keep out thoughts you have dismissed from your presence.

PUPIL: This making my mind do my new will is not going to be easy. I will practically have to make over completely my habitual mental processes.

MASTER: No, it will not be easy. But the goal the discipline will lead you to is worth a thousand times the effort required, however much effort that may be. If you will mentally stick tight to your resolve to make your mind a conscious center of divine operation, even for one week, seeing yourself growing steadily into what you wish to become, you will be amazed at your own growth and the genuine interest you have in everything around you. Also you will discover many, many wonderful things about yourself that you never knew before. Once you focus your attention and your intention on the Intelligent Life within you, and try to reproduce it in your own self, you will begin to get results that will seem almost phenomenal to you, and at once. Keep your consciousness focused on the fact that the Spirit of Life has no fears, no anxiety, and soon your feeling will correspond with It. Just try this, say for two weeks, without slipping; then ask yourself if you would go back to your old estate, if you could.

PUPIL: Is one apt to be "hypnotized," and thus hindered in progress, by the thoughts of others about one? Sometimes I seem to be making real progress when suddenly, and for no apparent reason, there is an almost uncontrollable impulse and feeling of "oh what is the use!"

I am like a ship without a rudder, trying to plow through some invisible, and invincible, force, and "getting nowhere fast," as the saying is.

At best these experiences are long, long detours off the main road. What causes these episodes?

MASTER: You gave it its right name in the beginning.

It is hypnotism; but as a rule it is self-hypnotism, almost unconsciously done because of the old habits of thought; and it comes as the result of your letting things other than your aim hold your attention.

Your efforts to control your thoughts should be steady, continuous, with no unguarded moments. Mere spasmodic efforts, however strongly indulged in at the times of their occurrence to you, will never take you very far on the road to the new goal you have set.

Before you study any further in these lessons, yes right now, make up your mind positively that you are entering upon the study to win, and that you will make an earnest, steady, continuous effort to do so. My own personal remedy for overcoming any tendency to slip back into the old rut of wrong thinking, and I assure you that I have always found it a most potent and sure panacea, is, believe it or not, that wonderful thing, derisively called "old-fashioned and out of date" by some, -The Lord's Prayer.

Go carefully over the Lord's Prayer every day.

If you do not already know it thoroughly, memorize it, so that you can repeat it anywhere, anytime, silently if you like.

Us it, repeat it carefully, slowly, and with much depth of feeling, as often as there is the least tendency to slip off your path. After you have finished with your reading, or repetition of the Prayer, then take up your mental picture again, mentally seeing, feeling, believing, knowing that you are already in possession of whatever it is that you want. This is what Jesus meant when He said for us to always, "ask believing that ye already have and ye shall have!" If you will do these things, very soon you will find that you ARE on the road to Freedom and Joy, and it will constantly grow easier for you to stay on the highway, without so many detours.

PUPIL: Just now I should like very much to have more money. In fact I must have it. Do you mean that I can attract the money I need by living with the Lord's Prayer for, say half an hour every morning and every night, just "precipitate" the money right out of the very air? That seems incredible!

MASTER: What you ask is incredible! And you are not getting my real meaning.

The finest statement of the Law of Life ever uttered is, in my opinion, that wonderful, wonderful statement of Jesus, namely: "Seek ye FIRST the kingdom of God and His righteousness (right-use-ness) and (then) all things will be added unto you."

But please note that first you must seek the kingdom, must make an honest effort to make your mind a center of divine operation only, and for its own sake and not from any ulterior motive. Then will all things be added unto you.

What happens to you through the steady, persistent use of the Lord's Prayer, as we were discussing it, is this: With the constant change in your mental attitude as you progress you are developing more and more strength and spiritual power. This self-mastery you are steadily developing is the growth of Divine Wisdom, Power and Beauty within you. Naturally then your whole outside world will gradually change to correspond to your new inside world because your most habitual thought takes outward form. Delightful changes will come into the circle of your individual world. Your thought and feeling will attract corresponding shapes; and you will feel much encouraged to go on and on and on into more and more joy and freedom.

Chapter 14

IMAGINATION AND INTUITION

MASTER: Today we shall discuss that great power we call imagination.

PUPIL: May I ask just what imagination is. I have heard you often speak of it as our "spiritual aeroplane," and say that "it wings us." But just what is it?

MASTER: No mortal can possibly answer that question. With all of our scientific research no one has found any rational clue as to the source of this great power, outside of God or Spirit. Nor has anyone been able to determine how far the use of imagination is able to carry one. It is Infinite. It is the mystery of mysteries; and it might be compared to electricity in this respect. Yet we know it does exist and that its power for good is inconceivable, if used constructively, correctly. What we should do is to inquire into its usefulness to us. Every normal person is equipped with it to some degree; and like the will the imagination can be developed. If rightly understood and correctly used it will perform seeming miracles.

PUPIL: But why do you call imagination the "spiritual aeroplane?"

MASTER: Because imagination, correctly used, can and will lift one, as if on wings, above and beyond all limitation, above one's low, narrow views of life, into a cloudless domain of true perspective. Imagination gives one clear vision of possibilities in your life which you have never been able to see before. Then while you realize that it takes determination and effort to achieve success; you also know that you can, with the imagination, tap the source of unlimited possibilities and Intelligent Energy. In a flash that mysterious, winged thing called imagination shows you where all the riches of Life are to be found.

PUPIL: Suppose one feels weak, obscure, poor, that you know your ideas are good but that you lack the money or health to carry them into effect. What can imagination do about these things?

MASTER: Imagination will reveal that strength and power and means are to be found within your Divine self and that a better and better acquaintance with, and a more frequent use of, the God-powers within is certain to lead to success on any line.

PUPIL: Can imagination lift one to great spiritual heights? Or does it pertain more to material success?

MASTER: Jesus, the Nazarene, lifted himself to the exalted Christhood through understanding and using his powers of imagination. Is that not reaching the heights spiritually?

PUPIL: Is it the imagination that opens the door for limitless good to enter?

MASTER: No, not correctly speaking.

It is intuition, a feminine, or soul, quality which first captures an idea from the Infinite and passes it on to the imagination.

Imagination raises one to a place in consciousness where all things are not only possible but are present, spiritual facts.

Look all about at the ones who have risen above every conceivable handicap to very great success.

Let us take Louis Pasteur, for example. He did not have any better mentality, or more strength, or more money, than any other ordinary Frenchman; and he was just as obscure as the lowest of them. His mental tools, by nature, were no sharper than yours are. But that strange and mysterious thing called imagination was very active in him and soared far beyond his scant equipment and early hardships into new realms of wisdom. Many times he was not sure; but he imagined; and because he imagined he discovered; and because he discovered he wrought miraculous cures and to this day his wisdom prevents disease and death in countless millions. Truly Pasteur was a saint.

The same is true of Paracelsus. People said he was lucky. Envious and lazy people always say this of anyone that succeeds. But the cures of Paracelsus were not luck; they were the result of his imagination and industry.

Jesus intimately acquainted himself with God through the use of his fertile imagination; and through use of the same mystic power he was able to enter into other lives. His success easily can be attributed to his ability to see God (which is Perfection) in every person he contacted, however tragic, lonely, hopeless or vicious that one seemed. Through his recognition of God in all men he helped men to see God in themselves. This was the source of his great power!

PUPIL: Then imagination is a veritable dynamo and not just a means of trivial, idle day-dreaming?

MASTER: Yes. Recognize your imagination as a dynamo of limitless power. Use all of it that you possess whenever you need it. Understanding of it, and experience in using it, will readily prove it to be the most powerful force in your mental equipment. Used correctly it will carry your light up among the brightest stars of highest heaven. It is not enough to dream and idly desire, not any more than it is enough to start an aeroplane's motor just to watch the propeller go round and round. You must fuel your imagination with knowledge and purpose. You must take your bearings and hold your course. Risks, hardships, will be only still greater opportunities to use your imagination in your journey through the clouds.

PUPIL: All of this sounds very interesting and inspiring. But when I look about me and see the people who are succeeding, and who have so much more in life than I have, it is confusing. They do not seem to know, or care, a thing about God. How about that?

MASTER: If I were you I would try attending to my own knitting and start at once to develop my own power; also I would stop envying others their success.

PUPIL: Oh I am not envying anybody anything. I simply do not understand.

MASTER: It would help if you would try to avoid a tailspin of self-pity. As soon as you observe someone who is getting on better than you are you must project yourself into his life critically. Try doing this same thing constructively. Explore his tactics, his tastes, his imagination and industry; and then ask yourself if you might not get along better and faster if you adopted some of the means he employs.

PUPIL: How can I know how another does his work to succeed? And I did not realize that I have been feeling sorry for myself. How would it be to try to see myself as others see me?

MASTER: It would help very much if you will turn your imagination on yourself without any excuses or alibis. Your imagination will show you your true self if you have the courage to use it and trust it. And let you intuition help you also.

Chapter 15

HUSBANDS, WIVES, CHILDREN AND WILLS

(Children, How to Bring Them Forth If You Wish Them, Home, Husbands, Wives, if You Desire Them.)

PUPIL: It seems to me that many of my married friends would be perfectly happy if only children would come to them. It seems strange they can not have any.

MASTER: No, it is not strange. It is all according to Law. "Principle is not governed by precedent." Children are the result of knowing, feeling, living that Law consciously or unconsciously; they are the birth of new ideas, something different.

Every baby is a new idea, a new form in which Life lives. Get into the habit of developing new ideas and you will find these very ideas taking the form of children. It need not matter what the new ideas are about so long as you fully develop them. Then mentally picture as many children as you would like to have. When about to give birth to the new idea in form (a baby) I would suggest the daily help of a really good Mental Science practitioner, also at the time of birth.

With proper understanding the birth of the child will be as natural as the spiritual idea which preceded the form.

PUPIL: All of this sounds very wonderful and convincing while I talk with you. At the risk of your thinking my mind a sieve may I ask you to put all three steps, husband, home, children, into concise, separate form.

MASTER: Very well. The idea of concentration is not a leaky one and I shall be happy to present them in the order you name. But first what, exactly what, does the word husband mean to you? What characteristics do you wish the husband to manifest? What should his disposition be in order to be in tune with yours? These are your very first steps along the way.

PUPIL: To me husband symbolizes certain characteristics I would like to attract to myself from the masculine side of Life, or quality of Life, a type of man I admire. His main qualities should be, for me, understanding and love. With these two attributes well-developed in both of us I believe happiness would be certain to follow.

MASTER: With love and understanding well developed in husband and wife happiness is certain to follow. The one certain way to attract this type of husband is to develop love and understanding in your self. It is a very great truth that like attracts like! So first think over carefully just the type of man you feel could be happy with you.

PUPIL: Oh, I thought I was to think of the qualities my husband should have to make me happy.

MASTER: That method would help to develop self-centeredness, selfishness. But the other way is a reaching out to GIVE what you have and has a very great attracting power. When you have determined the type of man whom you feel would be happy with you, then take for yourself an early morning-hour and through reading and meditation think yourself into the quality of Life you wish to attract and hold the feeling. Herein lies the real value of holding your thought and feeling into place, just like plugging into the light socket when you want light. If you keep pulling the plug you will not get much light. The secret is: MAKE your contact in thought and feeling and HOLD IT, with a happy, expectant attitude. Of course this ability to hold an idea is arrived at by developing the will.

PUPIL: It seems to me that visualizing will not work unless the mental pictures made are held in place in mind. Is that right?

MASTER: That is exactly right. They must be held in place, again just like the electric contact for lights must be held in place if you are to benefit by the light which will then stay on. Your magnet of thought and feeling draws from out of the whole Universe such qualities as Love, Understanding, Protection, Provision, husband, children, whatever it is you have visualized.

PUPIL: It is like a postage-stamp then; it only has value if it sticks. Am I right about this: that what I really AM that I attract? Might this not be the meaning of Jesus' statement in Matthew 13:20 when he said "For whomsoever hath to him shall be given and he shall have more abundance; but whosoever hath not from him shall be taken away even that which he hath?" When one really HAS a husband in feeling and mentally pictures him one really does HAVE that husband; and he is sure to appear in form as a human being: Is this not having more abundance? How slowly I grow. First I wanted my husband to have understanding; now I see that he IS understanding.

MASTER: That is it. Every conceivable thing that the human mind and heart can desire is already in existence. Like the electricity it has always been there; and as soon as one realizes it and tunes the desire in with that quality of Life which it is the current begins to flow in that direction. Then one has real abundance through continually having the recognition that whatsoever he may want he already has it.

PUPIL: Is the process the same if one wants several children?

MASTER: Yes, fundamentally it is the same. If we wish to manifest our new ideas of Life in the form of children, it is necessary to make the desire known to God, the Great, Ever-Present, Formative, Responsive, Creative, Intelligent Power. It being Responsive and Creative it manifests in form, as children.

PUPIL: Just what should one first begin to think and feel?

MASTER: First, let us suppose that your desire for children is in perfect accord with the Divine Plan to bring into earth existence a continual advancement of the human race. So your idea of the new birth is that you may be a means, or a channel, through which the All-Creating Principle of Intelligent, Beautiful, Perfect Life may reproduce Itself in a new form, one capable of recognizing itself as an individualized action of Pure Spirit. Then by reading good articles or books or by meditating on an affirmation that appeals to you, you tune your thought and feeling in with the very highest rate of vibration. Stay with the thought and feeling until you are certain that you HAVE made your contact with the Divine Intelligence, just as you are certain that you shall turn on the light when you plug into a light-socket. You know, under the latter circumstance, that the contact IS made because the room is flooded with light. And in the mental instance you know your contact IS made because your whole feeling IS flooded with certainty and a sense of security in God's Love and Power as they manifest in and through you.

PUPIL: It seems to me that one would have to keep constantly in mind the thought of begetting perfect ideas relative to every act.

MASTER: Jesus said: "Watch and pray lest you enter into temptation." You feel towards God (Life) in the same way your child feels toward you. If you obey the Laws of Life because you love your Father (Life) your child will do the same.

PUPIL: Is it necessary that both father and mother should desire the children? Should they take their meditations together? Should they discuss the hope of children?

MASTER: If both father and mother desire children the new idea will be a more perfect idea of God. It is not necessary to take the meditations together, in fact, I personally prefer to have all of my meditations alone. And it seems to me the less one discusses a desire with anyone the more quickly and perfectly the desire manifests. If one talks about a thing usually it is put in the future and is rarely discussed as a present fact; hence the manifestation is delayed indefinitely because of the habit of looking upon it as a future manifestation, as something that "will be" rather than something that is.

PUPIL: How is this for a method of bringing children of your own into one's personal life? First, study and think over the fundamental Law of Life as always giving expression to its highest ideals and ideas in human form. Man is God's highest ideal and the children of men are specialized ideas of the One Great Creative Source of all things. Are not our children the results of God's ideas of giving birth to our highest desires?

MASTER: You have the right idea. Try to really feel that God, Life, Love, Wisdom, is giving birth to a particular idea through you. Plant that idea, that thought-seed, in the garden of your individual subconscious mind. By using your individual subconscious quality of mind in this way you are doing your part to let all the Creative Energy in the Universe act in and through you without limit. Thus you are a bridge between the two extremes in the scale of Nature, one of which is the innermost Creative Spirit of Life and the other the particular, external form of a child. Your objective quality of thought power mentally sees your perfect child, then passes the thought and the picture into the creative power of your individual quality of subconscious mind which in turn transfers the thought-seed into ALL of the growing power there is in Life, thus bridging the two extremes of Nature. Your thought-seed will grow into perfect externalization just as a kernel of corn will when planted under the proper conditions.

PUPIL: This idea of a thought-seed clears up the whole Idea that my individual subconscious mind is the bridge between myself and the whole vast sea of Life.

MASTER: If you plant a kernel of corn you first make sure the soil and the climate is the proper kind to grow corn.

PUPIL: Does that mean I should look into my own character and physical condition, and so forth, to determine if I really am the type of woman to bear perfect children?

MASTER: You are right. It is vitally important to know these things. Once you have found out that these are clear, and you and your husband are sure in your minds that you wish to create in form your highest ideal of Love, as children, then proceed. Remember that the seed you plant, having all the vitality, all the vital essence, necessary to draw to itself from out of All Life every element necessary to cause it to grow into a perfect outward reproduction, a perfect child. Every parent, or parent-to-be, should be an enlightened parent, of course, and should do all within the power to bring forth, cherish, nurture and rear, the finest children possible. It will help those who are, or who desire to be, parents if they will inform themselves fully along the most scientific lines on this question. This they may do in numerous ways, through the reading of good books on the subject, ones that are written by specialists, also by taking courses on the subject that are offered almost continually through university-extension plans, also in many places by city and state departments; and lastly to seek the advice and care of the best physicians from conception forward.

Chapter 16

LIFE, LOVE, BEAUTY

MASTER: In his wonderful books Judge Troward stresses often that the Spirit of Life also is one of Love and Beauty, and that where the One is the others will be found, too, as a matter of necessity. Where Life is Love is. One is the correlative of the other. Where Life and Love are Beauty must be.

PUPIL: May we have another illustration to clarify this?

MASTER: Certainly. All persons have an appreciation of art. The ancient Greeks were supreme in the arts for many centuries. To this day many of their works have never been equaled. I have never seen that fact more compellingly illustrated than it was one day last summer at our home on The Esplanade, Redondo Beach, California. A gentleman friend of Mr. Smith's (Worth Smith, my husband) who, like Mr. Smith, has been a student of the Great Pyramid for many years, called on us. He brought a wonderful book and showed us many lovely pictures of exquisite Greek vases.

Alongside each photograph was a sketch of the same vase with the basic design highlighted in geometry, many lines drawn to salient features of the sketch. Of all the grace and beauty and absolute perfection of symmetry I have ever seen, or hope to, those pictures and sketches had it, without a solitary flaw in any of them. Each was purest harmony, so much so that one marveled and it seemed that music itself flowed from them. Each vase was an expression of God and His laws of Life, Love, Beauty and Harmony, executed to perfection by artists in whom His Love, Beauty, Harmony lived.

Because of their adoration of Beauty, and its Source in the Father, they were able to conceive Beauty in the mind when planning the designs of the vases. No doubt they sketched the designs as shown in the book, by employment of the geometry in which they excelled. With the model before them they then fashioned the works of superb Harmony to glorify the earth. Wherever perfect Harmony is there you will find perfect Love for they are twin blessings!

PUPIL: But all of us can not make such masterpieces, you know, for all of us do not have such artistic talents. Do we?

MASTER: All of us have some talent within us. Unfortunately, many seem to never realize it and never do anything about it. Even so any person of intelligence can put into whatever task that one may have to do the Spirit of Life, Love, Beauty and Harmony, IF only one will, and can make of the fruits of the task many things of Beauty. Some housewives, for example, make of housekeeping and rearing children a thing of drudgery as a result of their lack of illumination about the true divinity of housekeeping. Others put Love, Beauty, Harmony, Order and Joy into the same task and make a glory of it. It is a matter of the spiritual consciousness one has, or acquires through study if it is not there innately.

PUPIL: Will you please cite an example from the Bible which features this matter of consciousness of our divinity as being the root of all blessings?

MASTER: Gladly indeed. Study carefully St. Matthew, chapter 13, verse 12. Jesus uttered those golden words to teach mankind that like does attract like, invariably and infallibly. That passage states the law of attraction at its best, including an unshakable faith, visualizing by means of which one HAS spiritually, or in the mind, even that which is sought, and which serves as a magnet of infinite power to draw to one the glad fulfillment in form, or physical reality, provided only one also WORKS confidently and happily to carry out the ideas the Father gives one, through intuition, as steps in the path to the shining goal. Now let us directly quote the passage, then strip it bare of all the "mystery" so many claim it contains for them. Unfortunately, to many that verse remains a riddle for life unless they are sufficiently interested to seek until they find the key to its solution. The passage reads: "For whosoever hath, to him shall be given, and he shall have more abundance: but whosoever hath not from him shall be taken away even that he hath." The big question is:

"For whosoever hath" what? Does it mean the one who has wealth of money, or property, or other earthly possessions?

No, although the one who has the thing that is meant is certain to acquire financial independence and retain it. It means simply that "whosoever hath" the consciousness of the Father within, who has that exalted awareness as an abiding conviction, who has implicit faith in it, and who actively carries on in the work that one does, whatever it may be, the ideas of Life, Love, Beauty and Harmony the Father gives that one in an unending stream, to that one will be given all he may ever require, and to spare. But the person who "hath not" the high consciousness is subject to all the sorrows, lacks and other inharmonies circumstances and conditions can bring to bear upon him, even to the point of losing all he has gained through habitual employment of secondary causation. . . for since he has not the awareness he is, or shall be, "under the rule of an iron destiny," to quote Troward, and dwells in anxiety and fear, knowing not that "the eternal God is our refuge and a very present help in trouble."

PUPIL: Can that Love, Beauty and Harmony be caused to flow from one person, a practitioner let us say, into and through another so that the second party will be aware of the spiritual uplift, and receive corresponding benefits?

MASTER: Yes, indeed, that is done easily. That is the mission of the practitioner, for he or she does these things for others many hours a day. I well recall an incident that occurred not long ago in the beautiful home of a dearly beloved friend and student in Denver. I was sitting with her privately in her lovely living-room, holding her left hand in my right, thus completing a circuit exactly as an electric circuit is made, positive pole in contact with the negative pole. With my mind I made contact with the Love, Beauty and Harmony the Spirit is. From the Universal Spirit of Life those qualities flowed into me, and through me into my dear friend, and through her back into the Universal. For minutes we kept the contact and both of us were aware of the surge of tremendous power flowing through us. I have this friend's kind permission to mention her name. She is Grace N. Northcutt. It is she whose gracious generosity accounts for the new edition of this book you are now reading.

PUPIL: Then it is true that as one makes of it a habit to consciously recognize God in one's daily, hourly, even minute-byminute living in that degree one will get good results?

MASTER: Yes. The correspondence is exact! As we apply the laws of electricity we are certain to get results that correspond to those laws only. It is folly to apply one set of creative laws to a problem and expect to get results that correspond to a different code. So it is that if we set in motion through concentrated and consecrated thinking the laws of Harmony then only Harmony will manifest in and through us, and in our affairs! Again I give you the golden key which will unlock any door of bondage and which will never disappoint you if you persist in the use of it in wisdom. It is, I repeat, that twelfth verse of the thirteen chapter of Matthew.

PUPIL: How is it obtained? What price does one have to pay for the key?

MASTER: The price is given in the fifteenth chapter of John and is, as Jesus said: "Abide in me!" That will put you in an entirely new relationship to your Father and to your environment, will open up many new possibilities hitherto undreamed of, all by an orderly sequence of creative laws that result from your new mental attitude. Thought is the energy by which the law of attraction is brought into operation. It is by thought that we keep the sap of life flowing from the trunk into the branches. The statement Jesus made in Matthew 13:12 is so important that He made it repeatedly, worded a bit differently, yet containing the self-same law He expressed therein.

PUPIL: May we have a schedule, and some affirmations, for daily use? If we have one before us, in print, it should help a lot, it seems to me, in our follow-through.

MASTER First I shall give you two affirmations I have found very effective and powerful when consistently used with profound feeling.

1. "Father, I thank Thee for the conscious knowledge that all my good comes from Thee only, and that I no longer look to man as the source of my supply!"

2. "God IS my ever-present supply and large sums of money come to me quickly, under grace and in perfect ways, so to bountifully supply my every need, and to spare!"

Moreover a careful study of these three references will be a great aid, i.e., Mark 5:36 and 9:23, John 20:29. Lastly, I am happy to give you an excellent routine for daily use that Troward himself gave to me. I have used it faithfully for thirtyfive years now and it is a powerful help indeed.

It is this:

MONDAY - Watch your words!

TUESDAY - Watch your feeling!

WEDNESDAY - Watch your acts!

THURSDAY - Watch your receiving!

FRIDAY - Watch your giving!

SATURDAY - Look for the Spirit of Life and Love in everybody and in everything!

SUNDAY - Let the Lord's Prayer abide with you continually!

Attaining Your Heart's Desire

Foreword

"All we have willed or hoped or dreamed of good, shall exist, not its semblance, but itself."

Browning.

The thing that which hath been, it is that which shall be; and that which is done is that which shall be done.

Ecclesiastes 1:9.

The sages of the centuries, each one tincturing their thought with their own soul essence, have united in telling us that, "As a man thinketh in his heart, so is he."

It has been established by the experience of the ages that always the law is the same. But HOW shall one think in their heart, so that only goodness may blossom and ripen into rich deed and rare result?

What is the apparently mysterious secret by which life's dull metal is transmuted into precious mintage?

It is my purpose to tell you in this little book.

I desire to crystallize the heart-coinings of my revered master, Judge Thomas T. Troward, as reflected through the mirror of my mind and soul.

I have adopted as my means of expression, the dialogue style familiar to all students of that greatest of all speculative philosophers, Plato. I am convinced, through years of study of this almost superhuman mind, that this literary form is the one most nearly calculated to convey the most subtle shades of meaning, the richest depth of soul- sounding.

I know that my readers will agree with me that if they will put themselves in my place, as students, and let me answer them as my master answered me, it will clarify their interest and intensify their joy in these lessons.

What I wish particularly to convey to you within these pages is the method of scientific right thinking, and to awaken in you the desire to try to use this method in order to form the habit of thinking ONLY the thoughts you wish to see crystallized in a worthy achievement or result.

In addition, I want to direct your thoughts toward a better understanding of that Spirit of God, or Good, which points the way to the roseate dawn of a new civilization. The rapidity with which the ideas of man are changing causes humanity to realize that this new civilization is already manifesting itself through a clearer understanding of the relation between man and his Maker.

The epochal keynote of the present generation is that mind is the kingdom in which man reigns supreme.

As the poet says, "A brute I might have been, but I would not sink I' the scale." In endeavoring to make conscious use of thought-power, causing it to produce desired material results, mankind is beginning to understand the indispensability of absolute control.

My chief idea in sending forth this message is to make it easier for you to live in hourly consciousness that you have been given dominion over every adverse circumstance and condition which may arise.

The conscious use of the creative power of thought to protect and guide you, as well as to provide for you, is only attainable through understanding the "natural relations between mental action and material conditions."

Your reading of these lessons should be with a steadfast determination to think rationally and effectively on every word, in order that the full meaning of each thought may be thoroughly grasped and comprehended.

Thought-power is the kingdom of God in us, always creating results in our physical forms corresponding to our normal sustained thought.

As Troward has said,

"Thought is the only action of the mind. By your habitual thoughts you create corresponding external physical conditions, because you thereby create the nucleus which attracts to itself its own correspondence, in due order, until the finished work is manifested on the material plane."

This is the principle upon which we shall proceed to work out a simple and rational basis of thought and action whereby we may bring into outer expression any desired goal. Let us work together to this end.

Genevieve Behrend

Judge Thomas T. Troward, Philosopher and Sage

One of the really great minds and souls of modern times - and indeed of any time - was Thomas Troward, late Divisional Judge of the Punjab, India. Of his writings, the late William James of Harvard said, "Far and away the ablest statement of that psychology that I have ever met, beautiful in its sustained clearness of thought and style, a really classic statement."

The Boston Transcript editorially stated, "The author reveals himself as easily the profoundest thinker we have ever met on this subject." The late Archdeacon Wilberforce, when writing to Troward, signed himself, "Your grateful pupil." Responding to the many requests from Troward's friends and admirers for a more intimate glimpse of this great man, I am pleased to present to you a few phases of his daily life as I saw them while studying with him.

These may be all the more interesting because of the fact that I enjoyed the unique privilege of being the only pupil to whom he ever gave personal instruction.

The Early Life of a Genius

Thomas Troward was born in Ceylon, India, in the year 1847, of English parents and Huguenot ancestors.

When quite a young boy he was sent to England to be educated at Burmshtead Grammar School, but was most unhappy there, as he could not fully adapt himself to the humdrum life of the English schoolboy. Later on, when he continued his education in the beautiful Isle of Jersey, its charm entered into his blood, and he was thoroughly contented there.

Perhaps the old Huguenot strain in him found a congenial element in the semi-French environment of the college. At the early age of eighteen the natural bent of his mind began to assert itself, and he won the Helford College gold medal for literature.

When his studies were completed, Troward went up to London for the Indian Civil Service examination, a very stiff one, which he passed with high credit. He returned to India at the age of twenty-two in the capacity of Assistant Commissioner.

An incident which occurred during the course of his examination foreshadowed the trend of the life that was to replace the regulation judicial career when the twenty-five years of service had expired.

"Your Head is No Common One, Young Man"

One of the subjects, left for the end of the examination, was metaphysics.

Troward was quite unprepared for this, having had no time for research and no knowledge of what books to read on the subject, so he meditated upon it in the early hours of the morning, and filled in the paper with his own speculations.

The examiner, on reading it, was amazed, and asked "What text-book did you use for this paper?" "I had no text-book sir." Troward answered. "I wrote it out of my head." "Well, then, young man," was the examiner's comment, "your head is no common one, and if I am not mistaken, we shall hear from you again."

During Troward's career in India his official work kept him very busy. His recreation was often spent with canvas, paints and brushes.

He was an artist of no mean ability, especially in marine subjects, and had won several prizes at art exhibits in England. He loved to study the tombs of sacred Indian lore, or the scriptures of the Hebrews and of other ancient peoples.

While studying these profound subjects, there was unfolded to him, as in a vision, a system of philosophy which carried with it not only peace of mind, but also physical results in health and happiness.

When relieved of his burdensome official duties in the Indian Court, he returned to England, where a manuscript of some hundred folios slowly came into existence.

At that time he had no knowledge of Mental Science, Christian Science, New Thought, or any of the "isms" of modern thought.

His views were the result of solitary meditation and a deep study of the scriptures. The first edition of the now famous "Edinburgh Lectures" was published in 1904.

It was received with the almost unanimous opinion that its value could not be over-estimated, as was true of his subsequent volumes.

"Bible Mystery and Bible Meaning" proved especially attractive to churchmen. His books, by sheer worth, have found their way almost all over the world. In the United States alone, more than 50,000 copies have been sold.

Perhaps no one was more astonished at their warm reception than their simple-hearted, fun-loving author.

An Intimate Description

In physique Judge Troward was not the usual English type, but was more like a Frenchman, of medium stature, and not over five feet six or seven inches. He was dark complexioned, with small, bright eyes, a large nose, and a broad forehead.

When I knew him, he had a drooping mustache sprinkled with grey. He had the bearing of a student and a thinker, as is indicated in his writings.

His manner was simple and natural, and he exemplified a spirit of moderation in all things. I never saw him impatient or heard him express an unkind word, and with his family he was always gentle and considerate.

He seemed to depend entirely upon Mrs. Troward for the household management.

Only in the intimacy of his home did he entirely reveal his charming geniality and radiating friendship. His after-dinner manner was one of quiet levity and a twinkling humor.

He would enter into the conversations or parlor games of the family with the spirit of a boy. He did not care for public amusements.

One evening, after an excellent dinner of soup, joint of lamb, vegetables, salad, dessert, and wine, he rolled a cigarette, and, to my great surprise, offered it to me with the query, "Do you smoke?" Receiving a negative reply, he began to smoke it himself.

Noticing my poorly concealed expression of surprise, he remarked, "Why should you be shocked at anything which you can thank God for? I can thank God for one cigarette after, possibly a second, but never a third."

After he had finished his smoke, his youngest daughter, Budeia, played the violin for us. I observed that he became completely absorbed in the beautiful harmony. He told me afterwards that, although he was intensely fond of listening to music, he was in no sense a musician.

Although Troward did not indulge in outdoor sports, he loved nature, and would sit for hours by the sea with his sketch- book, or tramp the lonely moors in solitary meditation.

He said there were times when he obtained his best inspirations while walking in the open. He often invited me to go with him, although frequently he seemed to be unconscious of my presence, being entirely absorbed in his own thoughts.

Truth from the Trance

At times he would lapse into a trancelike swoon (his Maltese cat on the table by his side), the swoon sometimes lasting for hours.

At such times the members of his family would take particular care not to disturb him. When he emerged from these lapses of the senses, he would write down the truths which had been revealed to him.

Once he wrote on his memorandum pad,

"'I AM' is the word of power. If you think your thought is powerful, your thought is powerful."

It may be interesting to recall that such authorities as Barnett and the new American Encyclopedia, in their biography of Socrates, mention similar trancelike experiences of his.

While serving in the Greek army, Socrates suddenly found his feet seemingly rooted to the earth, where he remained in a trance for twenty-four hours. He awakened with a spiritual knowledge that transformed his life, and, later, the lives of many others.

The similarity of the life of this Athenian philosopher to that of Troward is that both relied chiefly upon intuition and common sense for their theory and system of living.

A difference between Troward's teaching and that of Christian Science is that he does not deny the existence of a material world.

On the contrary, he teaches that all physical existence is a concrete corresponding manifestation of the thought which gave it birth. One is a complement of the other.

I once asked him how one could impart to others the deep truths which he taught.

"By being them," he answered. "My motto is, 'Being, and not possessing, is the great joy of living.'"

Following a Trusted Guide

Judge Troward, although modest and retiring in his habits of speech and slow to express a personal opinion, was always willing to discuss any current subject, but extremely reticent and diffident about his own writings.

Never, to my knowledge, did he mention them unless approached on the subject. As a teacher, he was positive, direct, and always impersonal.

When our lesson was given indoors, he always sat in a large Morris chair, and, seeming not to be aware of my presence, he would think aloud.

To follow his thought was like following a trusted guide through the most difficult places, the darkest and least explored regions of thought.

As I followed, the personality of the man became obscure, and I was only conscious of the clear, commanding voice, and the light of the inward torch which he bore.

It was beyond doubt quite natural that he who made so clear the true meaning of individuality should in his teaching betray little of the personal or emotional element.

After I had been carefully guided to the most comforting conclusions, in the same quiet, unassuming manner as in the beginning of our mental journey, my guide would gently remind me that he had given me a few suggestions which I might follow if I felt inclined, but which were offered only in the friendly spirit of a fellow-traveler.

He always tried to impress upon me that every effort to accomplish mental control (which, in turn, meant control of circumstances) should be undertaken with absolute confidence of success.

The length of a lesson depended upon my ability to absorb what he was telling me.

If he were convinced in fifteen or thirty minutes that I understood quite naturally the reason why, for example, "If a thing is true." There is a way in which it is true," that lesson was concluded.

If it took me an hour or more to get into the spirit of his thought, the lesson was prolonged.

At the end of a lesson he would quietly remark, "Never forget that 'seeking' has 'finding' as its correlative:

'knocking,' 'opening.'"

With this reassuring statement, he would light his lantern and step into the denseness of the night to walk three miles to his home.

A Home-Loving Philosopher

Being a home-loving man, Troward delighted in his flower garden, and in the intimacy of his home, which he had provided with every comfort. He particularly enjoyed the seclusion of his studio and study, which were arranged to meet his personal needs and moods. His studio was in the most remote part of the house, and here he would spend hours of relaxation with canvas and paints. His study, however, was on the ground floor, and to it he would retire for meditation and research, usually in the early hours of the morning. He rarely worked at night. He had spent the greater part of the day he died sketching out of doors. When he did not join his family at the dinner hour, Mrs. Troward went in search of him. She found him in his studio, fully dressed, lying on the sofa in a state of physical collapse. About an hour later he passed away. The doctor said that death was caused by hemorrhage of the brain. I am sure that Troward would have said, "I am simply passing from the limited to the unlimited." He died on May 16th, 1916, in his sixty-ninth year, on the same day that Archdeacon Wilberforce was laid at rest in Westminster Abbey. It was no ordinary link that bound these two men, as you will note in the reproduction of the letter that follows, Troward's last letter to me. Thomas Troward regarded death very much as he would regard traveling from one country to another. He remarked to me several times, that he was interested in the life beyond and was ready to go. His only concern seemed to be the sorrow that it would cause his wife and family. When the time came, his going was exactly what he would have wished it to be. I hope that these few intimate touches will give to Troward's friends and admirers the information they desire concerning him.

I will add a more personal touch for you by presenting herein one of his first letters to me with facsimile of his handwriting.

31 Stanwick Rd., West Kensington, 8th Nov. 1912

Dear Mrs. Swink,

I think I had better write you a few lines with regard to your proposed studies with me as I should be sorry for you to be under any misapprehension and so to suffer any disappointment.

I have studied the subject now for several years, and have a general acquaintance with the leading features of most of the systems which unfortunately occupy attention in many circles at the present time, such as Theosophy, the Tarot, the Kabala, and the like, and I have no hesitation in saying that to the best of my judgment all sorts and descriptions of so-called occult study are in direct opposition to the real Life-giving Truth; and therefore you must not expect any teaching on such lines as these.

We hear a great deal in these days about "Initiation"; but, believe me, the more you try to become a so-called "Initiate" the further you will put yourself from Living Life.

I speak after many years of careful study and consideration when I say that the Bible and its Revelation of Christ is the one thing really worth studying, and that is a subject large enough in all conscience, embracing as it does our outward life of everyday concerns, and also the inner springs of our life and all that we can in general terms conceive of the life in the unseen after putting off the body at death.

You have expressed a very great degree of confidence in my teaching, and if your confidence is such that you wish, as you say, to put yourself entirely under my guidance I can only accept it as a very serious responsibility, and should have to ask you to exhibit that confidence by refusing to look into such so-called "mysteries" as I would forbid you to look into.

I am speaking from experience; but the result will be that much of my teaching will appear to be very simple, perhaps to some extent dogmatic, and you will say you had heard much of it before.

Faith in God, Prayer and Worship, Approach to the Father through Christ --all this is in a certain sense familiar to you; and all I can hope to do is perhaps to throw a little more light on these subjects, so that they become to you, not merely traditional words, but present living facts.

I have been thus explicit, as I do not want you to have any disappointment; and also I should say that our so-called "studies" will be only friendly conversations at such times as we can fit them in, either you coming to our house or I to yours as may be most convenient at the time.

Also I will lend you some books which will be helpful, but they are very few and in no sense "occult."

Now if all this falls in with your own ideas, we shall, I am sure, be very glad to see you at Ruan Manor, and you will find that the residents there, though few, are very friendly and the neighborhood is pretty.

But on the other hand if you feel that you want some other sort of learning, do not mind saying so; only you will never find any substitute for Christ.

I trust you will not mind my writing to you like this, but I don't want you to come all the way down to Cornwall and then be disappointed.

With kind regards

Yours sincerely,

(Signed)
T. Troward

Lesson I

Interpreting the Word

Feeling that an explanation of some of the words employed in an unusual way in these lessons may be helpful to the student, I herein offer a list of such words, together with my interpretation and references from Troward.

Absolute

"That which is free from limit, restriction, or qualification." (Webster.) "An idea from which the elements of time and space are entirely absent." (Troward.)

Example: Thinking in the absolute would be simply dwelling upon the intrinsic qualities of love without reference to whom you love or the various forms through which love expresses itself.

Mind is absolute because of its self-reaction.

Being

Life, that unformed power of life which controls circumstances and conditions. Read Troward's "Bible Meaning and Bible Mystery," pages 77-79.

Belief

A certain quality in the creative power of thought, which manifests on the external plane in exact correspondence to the quality of belief entertained.

If you believe that your body is subject to disease, then the creative power of thought of disease results in a diseased body.

Read Troward's "Edinburgh Lectures of Mental Science," page 14.

Body

The instrument through which thoughts and feelings are expressed. The envelope of the soul.

Brain

The instrument through and in which the action of the Universal Parent Mind expresses itself in specific form as individual thoughts.

Brain is not the mind, but the mind's instrument.

Christ

A State of consciousness which is altogether good, and a quality of feeling which manifests in physical form. The most perfect spiritual concept.

Circumstances

The outward effect which corresponds to the inward tendency of thought.

Conception

William James says "...denotes neither the mental state nor what the mental state signifies, but the relation between the two."

Concentration

"Bringing the mind into a condition of equilibrium which enables us to consciously direct the flow of spirit to a definite, recognized purpose and then carefully to guard our thoughts from inducing a flow in the opposite direction." - Edinburgh Lectures of Mental Science. Page 88. (Troward.)

Conditions

The result of mental tendencies. Harmonious thought produces harmonious physical and material conditions, which still further react to sweeten thought.

Consciousness

Activity of mind which enables it to distinguish itself from the physical form in which it manifests.

Create

To bring into existence. Thought is creative, because it always brings into physical or objective existence forms which correspond to itself.

Death

Absence of life. Loss of consciousness, with no capacity to regain it. Example: If a thought has been absolutely eliminated from the consciousness and cannot be recalled, it is dead to you.

Faith

"The divine promises and individual faith are correlations." Combine them, and there is no limit to what you can do through the creative power in this quality of thought." Essential thought.

Therefore every call to have faith in God is a call to have faith in the power of your own thought about God." (Troward)

A confident expectant attitude of mind. Such a mental attitude renders your mind receptive to the creative action of the spirit of life. Have faith in the force of your own thought.

You have many times experienced what it will do. Jesus' statement, "Have faith in God and nothing shall be impossible unto you." is not a mere figure of speech; it is a scientific fact, simply stated. Your individual thought is the specialized working of the creative power of life. (All Life.)

Intelligence

The Universal Infinite Mind. The highest intelligence is that mind which understands itself as the instrument through which the Intelligence which brought it into existence operates.

Love

Universal Life and Universal Law are one.

The law of your being (your life) is that you are made in the image of God (the Creative Power which brought you into existence) because you are God's very self specialized.

The law of your life is that your mind is "the individualization of Universal Mind at the state of self-evolution in which your mind attains the capacity for reasoning from the seen to the unseen and thus penetrating behind the veil of outward appearance.

So because of the reproduction of the divine creative faculty in yourself, your mental states or modes of thought are bound to externalize themselves in your body and in your circumstances." (Troward.)

Spirit

It is impossible to analyze the nature of Spirit (or Life), but we can realize that whatever else Spirit may be, it is a self- creating power which acts and reacts upon itself, reproducing itself in inconceivable forms from the cosmos to man.

(Just as your mind acts and reacts upon itself when you are memorizing.)

Origin of all visible things.

As it is independent of time and space, it must be pure thought, the embodiment of stored consciousness.

A self-acting and self-reacting non-physical creative power or force. Its action can only be thought because thought is the only conceivable non-physical action.

Thought

The specialized action of the original, creative Spirit or Mind.

Truth

That which lives in you is truth to you.

Visualizing

Inward or mental vision. (Visioning). Life's creating power taking particular form. The act of producing in your mind the picture of any contemplated idea.

Word

Your individual thought is the specialized word or action of the originating mind-power itself.

"That which starts the etheric vibration of life moving in a special direction," corresponding to the word, which originates special movement.

"The seed which gives rise to the thing." Plant your word- seed in the Subjective Mind of the universe, and you are sure to receive a corresponding thing, just as truly as poppy seed produces poppies.

Faith gives substance to things unseen. (The unseen word or thought.)

How to Get What you Want

Sage: If a thing is true, there is a definite way in which it is true. And the truest thing in Life is that it contains inherent within itself absolute joy and liberty of mind, body, and affairs.

Pupil: Do you mean that my understanding of Life's laws can give me the realization of perfect liberty in my individual life?

Sage: Yes, providing you do not make the common error of judging everything from a material standpoint only.

Recent research in physical science has established the fact that there is enough power in a lump of clay to destroy a city.

All the average mind is able to see is the inert clay, whereas, in reality, it is the physical instrument which contains the invisible power.

Pupil: Then when I understand the law of vibration, I can get anything I want; achieve anything I desire?

Sage: Life fills all space, and through the understanding and use of Life's laws, you can give direction to a particular quality of creative force, which, if held in place by the will, is absolutely certain to reproduce in a corresponding physical form.

What every human being wants is more liberty and more joy in life.

From whatever angle you study the subject of Life, you will find that degrees of livingness and liberty are invariably manifested by varying degrees of intelligence.

What you would term inanimate life represents the lower forms of intelligence; in plant life you recognize a higher degree of intelligence.

To illustrate this, look at a flower. Is it not beautiful? Does it not prove to you the indisputable presence of a Great Intelligence which is expressing itself as beauty, form, and color, and above all, joy?

Pupil: Yes.

Sage: Still you will not find it difficult to recognize in the animal kingdom a quality of Life and Intelligence which is greatly in advance of that manifested in the flower.

Then the intelligence which expresses itself in the mind of man as the power of initiative and selection is the highest expression of Intelligent Life. Thus you see that the inanimate, the plant, the animal, and the human all represent the same Universal Life, the only difference being in the varying degrees of intelligence.

For example: You are expressing a very high degree of intelligence in desiring to understand the laws of Life. When you have discovered some part of these laws, you will ascend the scale of intelligence as you make practical application of your discoveries.

Another example: Two men leave college with the same degrees and situated very similarly relative to social and financial position. Both study the laws of Mind; both are obliged to struggle.

One, by making a great mental effort, keeps mentally above the discouraging conditions, and finally becomes a smooth read, while the other one becomes disheartened and ill barely making out a miserable existence. You can readily see where the high form of intelligence was manifested in these two cases.

Intelligence was there, but it could only grow by being used constructively.

How Degrees of Intelligence Prove Man's Place in the Universe

Sage: The greater your intelligence, the more easily you can call into action the highest order of creative energy.

The more highly you develop your intelligence (and I do not mean by this intellectuality or book learning – I mean self- education) the more you will find your old limited ideas of what you are not, cannot be, do, or have, imperceptibly slipping away.

By using your intelligence and resting upon it to guide you Godward, you will come to recognize that you are as much a part of the very highest Intelligence as a drop of water in a part of the ocean.

This steady recognition on your part, carried into your everyday affairs, will give you control over adverse circumstances, which you realize are, after all, only effects of lower degrees of intelligence, and will deliver you from falling a victim of a material universe.

You are not a victim; you are a part of the Universe.

Pupil: Just what do you mean by "effects of lower degrees of intelligence?"

Sage: I mean, by a lower degree of intelligence, one that is unable to recognize itself as being one of the highest forms of life.

The highest degree of intelligence is that form of life which is able to recognize itself as related to all existing Intelligence.

For example: You can easily recall the last difficult situation you came through. It was the expression of the highest form of Intelligence which enabled you to think your way out of that.

Sage: You recognized your difficulty, but you also recognized your intelligence as being able to draw to itself, from out the whole Universe, ways and means of meeting that perplexing problem.

The Law is ever the same.

When you are convinced that every physical circumstances or thing has its origin in corresponding activities of the mind (thought), you are able to conquer adversity in any form, because you know you can always control your thoughts.

You must always be determined do to your own thinking.

Pupil: It is not difficult for me to understand that the flower is the result of some invisible power, which must be Intelligence, but for me to realize that this same life and intelligent power in my life is not easy.

I had not been taught to think in this way.

However, you have made me realize that if I wish to learn, I must put into practice the directions you have given me.

So when I needed to have five hundred dollars at a certain time and could not see any possible means of getting it, I tried to follow your instructions by mentally seeing myself as doing the thing I wished to do.

I visualized myself paying my obligation, and in some way, which is still a mystery, I was able to feel quite calm about it.

I made my mental picture and actually forgot to worry about the ways and means, and the money came. I did not quite understand then, and I do not know now, just how it happened.

All that I am able to realize is that, by my obedience to your teaching, the day was saved for me, and I shall not forget it.

Now I would like to know if we inherit our tendencies of mind?

Sage: Most of us inherit our thoughts, just as we inherit the color of our eyes.

If you intend to understand the relation existing between mental action and material conditions sufficiently well to control your circumstances, you must think for yourself, and in your own way, irrespective of what your ancestors thought, even though some of them might have brought desired results.

Pupil: That seems as impossible as reaching the horizon. However, if you tell me that I can arrive at the place where circumstances and conditions will be under my control, through a steady and determined effort to find out the truth along these lines, I shall do my own thinking from this moment.

My present condition, however, seems beyond the control of any human being, much less myself and there have been times when I did control certain conditions, but at other times the same conditions were beyond my control.

Why was that?

Sage: The reason you succeeded, without understanding the power which you possesses, was that you used it unconsciously, according to the law of its own nature, and reached harmonious results (as in the incident that you have just related).

Your ability, at all times, to use the unfailing power which is yours depends upon your recognition of its presence.

The reason for your times of failure is that the distressing condition so wholly absorbs your attention that you are unable to think of anything else.

At such times you entirely lose sight of the fact that your individual mind is the instrument through and in which the very highest form of intelligence and unfailing power is endeavoring to express itself.

Also, that it always takes the form of your habitual thought. Therefore, when you believe that a situation is beyond your control, so it is.

Pupil: Which means that my control of circumstances is entirely measured by my capacity to know that the life and intelligence in me is the same Life and Intelligence which brought me into existence?

The same Life in trees and all nature, and I tune in with all Life?

Will this steady recognition give me direct contact with all the power and intelligence which exists?

Would simply dwelling on this thought solve any situation which might arise?

Sage: No.

"Faith without works is dead."

God without expression is a nonentity.

Thought without action is powerless.

But your recognition that you are inseparably connected with the joy, life, intelligence, and power of the Great Whole, unwavering maintained and carried into practical application will solve any problem, because your thought calls into specific action ideas of the very highest degree of intelligence and power, which naturally controls the lesser degrees.

"The Lesser modes of life are in bondage to the law of their own being because they do not know the law."

Therefore, when you know the Laws of Life, this knowledge gives you ideas that enable you to control all adverse circumstances and conditions.

Pupil: This is all so new to me, I do not quite grasp your meaning. Will you please give me an illustration?

Sage: Well, suppose you were in a room where every comfort had been provided for you, but the room was in total darkness, and you were unable to locate the things you desired, although you were conscious of their presence.

You were told that the room was electrically lighted, and instinctively you began to grope your way along the wall, where you were accustomed to look for a light switch.

For hours you passed your hands up and down the walls as far as you could reach until you were quite fatigued.

You were about to give up the search and make the best of a bad situation, but, overlapping this thought, there came the resolve that you would not abandon your effort until you had located it.

You were determined to enjoy the good things awaiting you, so you renewed your search with the feeling of assurance that ultimately you would find a way to turn on the light.

After more fruitless endeavor, you paused to rest, and to wonder where that switch could possibly be, "It must be here, and I shall find it," you said to yourself, and again you passed your hands over the walls, although you felt certain that you had gone over every inch that you could reach. This time your thoughts and movements were not quite so tense, although equally determined.

As your hands moved slowly up and down, your mind caught the idea that the switch might not be on the wall at all. You paused a moment, and the suggestion that it might be on the floor registered in your consciousness. But reason stepped in and argued, "Impossible. Whoever heard of a light switch being placed on the floor!"

But, the suggestion persisted, "why not try"

You have gone over what first seemed the most reasonable places to find it. "Try the floor."

So then you began to reach out uncertainly with your feet for some projection on the floor which might be a light switch.

Almost instantly your feet came into contact with an unfamiliar object. You put your hand on what seemed to be a push button, but no light appeared.

Nevertheless, you now felt quite sure that you had located the switch. You paused, and involuntarily asked yourself, "How does this thing work? It won't push and it won't pull."

Back came the answer within yourself like a spoken word. "Sidewise." You moved it sidewise, and the room is flooded with light. Your joy at thus finding a responsive intelligence within yourself could not be expressed in words.

It was a rapture of the heart that many have felt at times.

Pupil: Oh, I am so glad that the switch was found through clinging to the right mental attitude! Does such persistent effort always meet with such a satisfactory reward?

Sage: Yes, persistent, confident endeavor always brings satisfaction.

In order to give you a complete picture from which you may logically reason in the future, let us consider the same situation from an opposite angle.

Imagine yourself in the same room under the same conditions. After several attempts at feeling around in the dark, you begin to feel tired, more or less discouraged, and you reason with yourself thus "Oh, what is the use? There may be a light switch in this room, and the room may contain everything I require, and again it may not."

But something indefinable in yourself convinces you that not only is the light there, but so, also, are the things you enjoy and desire. You answer right back to yourself, "Well, if everything is here which I need and would enjoy, what a pity that I cannot find the switch!

What a strange and unreasonable way some people have of doing things! I wonder why the light was not already turned on for me."

Pupil: You make it seem that one almost involuntarily and invariably blames circumstances or people for his failures.

"The Fault, Dear Brutus, Lies Not in the Stars, But in Ourselves, That We are Underlings"

Sage: You must admit that it is rare to find anyone who realizes that the cause of his failure or continued misfortune lies within himself.

The reason for this is an almost universal lack of understanding on the part of the individual that a certain quality of thought brings to the consciousness a recognition of an intelligent power capable of attracting to him, and directing him to, the fulfillment of his purpose and the attainment of his desire.

On the other hand, the inversion of this same power affects a negative result.

Pupil: You mean that a certain quality of thought enables one to do and be what he wishes, while the misuse of the same power seems to thwart one's purpose?

Sage: Yes. The idea is to use your power of thought and feeling positively, in order to attain positive results.

Use it negatively, and you get negative results, because the unchangeable law is,

"Intelligence always manifests in responsiveness."

The whole action of the evolutionary process of Life, from its first inanimate beginning up to its manifestation in human form, is one continual intelligent response.

If you would induce yourself to recognize the presence of a Universal Intelligence which permeates all nature, you must also recognize a corresponding hidden deep down in all things —in the trees, the weeds, and flowers, in the animals, and in fact, in everything —which is ever ready to spring into action when appealed to.

It will respond to your call as a child would obey when bidden to come and play.

In your first experience in the dark room, your all-absorbing thought was not so much about the darkness as about the light, and how it could be turned on.

The positive "I will" quality of your thought brought up from the depth of your inmost soul a steady flow of intelligent power, which finally penetrated through to your intellect and guided your hand to the switch.

Pupil: But the second time when I also thought I must find the switch, there was no enlightened response.

It seems to me that this is one's everyday experience. The first case seems like a miraculous coincidence.

Sage: Oh, no. All is Life, and all is law and order. There are no coincidences in reality, no "happen so's."

You will realize this if you will recall some of your own experiences similar to the ones used in the illustrations.

You often feel that you must have "light," and, after several attempts to avail yourself to it, your thought and feeling settle into the "I cannot do it" groove; "it may be possible for those who know how, but I don't," etc.

The best method of learning the truth about this is to live your past experiences over again. Analyze what your thoughts and feelings were when you succeeded, and when you failed. Then draw your own deductions. No written or spoken words equal this kind of instruction.

Remember that all space is filled with a responsive Intelligence and Power ever ready to take any form which your sustaining thought-demand creates.

This power can work only in terms of the thought instrument through which it operates. Humanity generally admits Jesus' ability, Jesus' power to use the spirit of intelligent life to produce material conditions —as in turning water into wine, but they doubt their ability to use the same Power in themselves, in spite of Jesus' assurance, "All things are possible unto you."

Now this statement is either true or false.

If true it is because your mind is the instrument in and through which this intel-ligent Principle of Life takes initiative action, and this action, in turn, is always in accordance with the laws of life, which are subjective in their nature.

Life's Greatest Purpose is to Express Joy, Beauty, and Power

Pupil: Am I right in concluding that this lesson in life, which is an ever-present, limitless, intelligent power, is ready at all times to be guided in any direction that my sustained thought may give it?

If I permit to be anxious, discouraged, dissatisfied, I bring into action repelling, destructive forces?

Life's purpose is to give expression to Its joy, beauty, and power, through Its particular instrument, my thought.

Is this right?

Sage: You have grasped the letter of the lesson in a remarkable way.

Now it remains only for you to experience the happiness of what you have learned.

Do this by putting your knowledge to practical application, never losing sight of the fact that no matter what justification you may think you have at the time, any feeling of discouragement, dissatisfaction, or anxiety causes the fulfillment of your right desire to recede further and further away from you.

Whereas, by persistent and determined endeavor to trust your own desires and ambitions as the specific expression of the universal loving, guiding, and protecting Principle, you will find that your supply for their fulfillment will unfold to you greater and greater liberty in every direction.

Pupil: When one does not wish to entertain negative thoughts, how can the sense of discouragement and anxiety be shut out?

I am sure that it is not because one enjoys feeling worried that it seems so difficult to eliminate it.

Do you mean that it is as possible to snap out of a thought one doesn't want as it is to step from one room to another?

I should like to know how that is accomplished, as I have many unwelcome thoughts which I am wholly unable to dismiss at the time.

After a period they leave, but it seems to me they use their own sweet will about it.

I have honestly tried to rid myself of thoughts, which seemed to cling all the tighter when I tried to throw them off. It would be wonderful to cast off a thought as one would a garment!

How can it be done?

Sage: By keeping a positive attitude of mind regarding your innermost desire as an accomplished fact, whether it be for a state of mind or for a thing.

You cannot think positive and negative thoughts at the same time.

Pupil: Oh, is that true? It seems to me I have often been speaking to someone on a certain subject while my thoughts were on an entirely different one.

You Can Actually Think of Only One Thing at a Time

Sage: You were thinking one thing and saying another. You had only one thought. You automatically said one thing while thinking another.

In short, your words were not the expression of the thought in your mind.

Suppose you give yourself a test; try to think of yourself as a success and a failure at the same time.

You will find it impossible to think positively and negatively simultaneously.

In our next lesson we will take this up more extensively and prove why it is true.

Also why you, as an individual, can control circumstances, whether they be mental, physical, or financial, through the understanding of your personal relationship to the Intelligence which governs the universe.

Pupil: I know that what you say is true, but just what method should I employ to accomplish this?

There are times when I become cross and impatient with myself because I give way to anxiety and fear (the very things which I know now will cause my defeat).

And yet I will do it, just as I will eat something I like even though I know it will disagree with me.

Could you give me a formula to use at such times?

Sage: When the triad of enemies—fear, anxiety, and discouragement—assails you, poisoning your mind and body, weakening your power to attract what you want, begin instantly to take deep breaths, and repeat as fast as you can, aloud or silently, the following affirmation, which is an antidote to the poison and a powerful assurance and attraction of Good:

"The Life in me is inseverably connected with all the life that exists, and it is entirely devoted to my personal advancement."

If you are alert and can make this affirmative thought overlap the negative, anxious suggestion, you will very soon free yourself.

If the tendency to dwell on these erroneous beliefs keeps recurring, go where you can be alone, repeat your affirmation, and endeavor to lift your mind up to your words, much as you would lift your breath from the bottom to the top of your lungs.

Never be impatient with yourself because you do not quite succeed in your every endeavor.

It is your intention that counts, not necessarily the absolute fulfillment of the letter.

The ALL-KNOWING POWER THAT IS understands and rewards accordingly. Be diligent and patient and you will surely succeed.

Lesson III

How to Overcome Adverse Conditions

"There is nothing either good or bad, but thinking makes it so."
--Shakespeare.

Sage: If you wish to overcome adverse conditions or to maintain a favorable one, it is necessary to have some knowledge of the fundamental or originating Spirit, and your relation to It.

The true order of these fundamental principles of life which you are endeavoring to understand does not require you to deny the reality of the existing physical world, or to call it an illusion.

On the contrary, by admitting the existence of the physical, you thereby see the completion of a great invisible, creative process.

This enables you to assign physical manifestations to their proper places in the creative series, which your former way of thinking did not enable you to do.

You now realize that, while the origin of life is not in itself physical or material, it must throw out physical and material vehicles through which to function as its means of expression, in varying degrees of intelligence, such as the vegetable or the animal kingdom, and the human, as illustrated in our last lesson.

All are forms of life, because of that inner Principle of being which sustains them. The Life Principle with which you are primarily concerned is the life of thought and feeling in yourself.

You are a vehicle or distributing medium of the creative Spirit of Life.

If you understand this, you will have some idea of what the originating Spirit of Life is in Itself, and your relation to It as an individual.

Pupil: Since thought and feeling are the origin of all things, would it not be necessary to get into the spirit of their origin in order to control circumstances?

Is it true that my thoughts and feelings are the same as those of the limitless Power and Intelligence of the universe?

Sage: In essence they are the same.

You are able to control the circumstances and conditions relative to your individual world, of which you are the center, by making your thoughts and feelings correspondent in quality (at least in a degree) to what you believe are those of the originating, intelligent forces of life.

Pupil: Is it true that the life in me contains everything that

I, as an individual, could ever require?

Are my thoughts and feelings the centralizing power of my particular world?

If so, then Browning explains the situation when he says, "We carry within us the wonders we seek without us."

If I know and practice this great fact, the wonder of Life's understanding power will come forth in me by its own divine right, and assume command over all my problems in exactly the same degree that I recognize it.

Is that correct?

Sage: Yes, Browning has voiced the truth in that sentence. The divine Principle in you is complete, and is the only Life there is.

But this should not lead you into the error of believing that you are not to exert yourself.

Remember that the life-germ in you is an Intelligence which can call into specific action all of life's forces from out the entire universe, but it can only work through your intelligence in correspondence to what you confidently believe it can and will do.

Therefore, be practical in your reasoning, and diligent in your deeds.

Suppose I give you an example:

You have a glass of dirty water. In order to have the clear water, you would continue to pour the clean water into the glass of dirty water until every drop of the dirty water had flowed out of it, wouldn't you?

The same rule applies to adverse conditions. Pour into them a steady stream of confidence in the power of God in you to change them, and they will change, correspondingly.

Pupil: I understand. You mean that I should use my common sense, coupled with a steady faith in God and earnest, concentrated mental effort?

Sage: That is it. Use your common sense and all your mental faculties as far as they will take you.

However, you should never try to force a situation. Always allow for the Law of Growth. Remember that conditions will grow into the correlative shape of your firmly held mental attitude "under the guidance of the All Creating Wisdom."

If you will follow this method of reasoning, you will soon form the habit of examining your own attitude of mind for the key to your progress and enjoyment of life.

Endeavor to keep before your mind's eye the thought that every physical or material condition in your life corresponds to your habitual thought tendency, and your thought tendency will eventually become the reproduction of the way you regard your personal life, as related to all life.

Pupil: Shall I be able to overcome one limitation after another, as I develop the knowledge and feeling of regarding the Life Principle in me as the source of all physical experience?

As I advance along these lines, shall I grow into the liberty of enjoying life in my own way?

Sage: In studying the law of your own being, the important thing to realize is that you, as an individual, are a specializing center, through which the power or essence of Life takes forms which correspond exactly to your most habitual conceptions.

Try to realize more and more thoroughly, both in theory and in practice, that the relation between your individual mind and the Universal Parent Mind is one of reciprocal action.

Grasp the principle of reciprocity, and you will comprehend why you fall short sometimes of enjoying life, and how you can attain to full enjoyment; just as the law of gravitation shows why iron sinks in water, and can also be made to float.

Pupil: It is rather difficult for me to understand what you mean by the reciprocal action between my individual mind and the Universal Parent Mind.

Suppose I am facing a big financial problem, and I endeavor to bring my mind into a state of confident expectancy through meditation upon the ever-present supply in all forms of life, and by repeating an affirmation which seems logical.

Would that do it? Where does the reaction come in? And how?

If my happiness in life depends upon this understanding, and upon living in a state of conscious reciprocity with the Parent Mind, it seems just now that it is a long way off, because I do not grasp your meaning.

Should I feel a reaction within myself when striving for a certain state of consciousness?

Sage: We said in our last lesson that your mind was at outcome of the great Universal Parent Mind which brought you into existence for the direct purpose of expressing Itself Through you. The reciprocal action between your mind and the Parent Mind might be compared with a tree and its branches.

Your mind is the specific expression of the Universal Mind from which it draws its power to think.

Just as a branch of a tree is a specific part of a tree, not apart from it, but a part of it.

Thus, between the Universal Mind or Life and its own specialized expression (which is your mind), there is a perpetual interaction, as with the tree and its parts; its branches and its leaves are continually drawing sustenance from the parent trunk.

Your thought action is the specialized, identical action of the Universal Mind.

Example: Imagine yourself feeling a bit downcast, when suddenly you are handed a telegram with the news that the one person in the world whom you love the most is on his way to see you, and the messenger of some wonderful news!

Can you not imagine what a definite reaction you would have from news like that!

Well, you can stimulate the same quality of thought, that same feeling of joy and surety between your individual mind and its source, through mentally picturing yourself as doing the things that you enjoy.

See yourself happy, and lift your mind up to it by constantly repeating a happy affirmation, and you will readily realize the reaction in kind.

Pupil: I see. The way that adverse conditions are to be overcome is through my recognition of the reciprocal action going on continually between my mind and the One great Universal Mind, which brings about the same kind of a reaction that I would have from an agreeable experience on the physical plane.

I used to think that conditions were overcome by ignoring them, and setting aside the inherent law that caused them.

I begin to realize now (theoretically at least) that the laws of life cannot be ignored nor destroyed, but, on the contrary, must be made to work for us to produce a harmonious existence.

Sage: Adverse circumstances are overcome by reversing the originating cause, which is your own thought.

Anxiety and fear always attract conditions of their own kind. Reverse this tendency and entertain only those thoughts which register harmony and confident assurance, and the adverse circumstances will recede, and in their place will appear the conditions which correspond to your changed mentality.

Pupil: Am I to regard my mind as a branch of the Universal

Mind from which I draw all my substance?

Sage: Yes. You now have a fairly good general idea of the two ultimates: the Universal and the individual, and their relation to each other.

I think we should now consider the process of specialization, that is, how to make nature's laws produce a particular effect which "could not be produced under the simple generic conditions spontaneously provided by nature."

How to Remedy Nature's Shortcomings

Pupil: How can one create conditions not provided by nature?

Sage: Do not overlook the word "spontaneous."

By consciously and intelligently arranging your thoughts in the new order, by looking within yourself for the solutions of your problems, instead of without, you will certainly find that ideas will come to you, which, if followed, will produce new conditions other than those provided by nature.

Pupil: How can I do this? Is this brought about by causing my thoughts to correspond to those which I think the Universal Mind must have?

Sage: Let me give you an illustration of what I mean.

Take the case of a miller who has been grinding his grain by hand.

His instinctive feeling is that there should be a more efficient way of grinding grain, and he meditates a good deal on what this way might be.

One day, while walking in the country, his attention is attracted, for the first time, to the power in a stream of water as it rushes past him. He pauses, and reflects on how this power could be utilized for his particular purpose.

"Why not harness it and make it grind my grain?" he asks himself.

This unexpected inspiration thrills him through and through, not only because of its possibilities, but because of his feeling of assurance that it can be accomplished. Immediately, the desired result begins to picture itself in his mind.

By the side of the stream he sees his gristmill working under conditions, with a great wheel attached to it revolved by the force of the running water, and thus grinding his grain.

The force of the water spontaneously provided by nature has not been changed; it has been specialized to meet an individual requirement.

How Nature Working Through Mind Can Grind the Grain

Pupil: Naturally the power of the water could not of itself have ground the grain, but through the interaction of the individualized Universal Intelligence in the miller's mind, he made this power "spontaneously provided by nature" do his bidding, just as Burbank specialized nature's laws by making cactus grow without thorns, and blackberries without seeds.

Sage: Yes, you have grasped my meaning.

Your comprehension of the interaction between the water- power, or nature, and the individualized Intelligence in the mind of man is scientifically correct.

You see now that it is an entire reversal of your old conception.

Formerly, you took forms and conditions as symbols, and inferred that they were the causes of mental states and material conditions; now you are learning that the true order of the creative process is exactly the reverse, that thought and feeling are the originating causes which form corresponding external conditions.

This is the foundation principle upon which you can specialize the generic law of the whole creative process, and cause it to bring all of its Intelligence and Power to bear, in meeting your particular necessity.

Pupil: You are right. I have been inverting the order of cause and effect.

It always seemed to me that conditions both created and controlled my thoughts, that is, I involuntarily accepted the thoughts which the conditions suggested.

For example: Suppose I want to be at a certain place at a certain time. My appointment is important and I shall be late.

What a terrible thing it will be! There seems nothing to be done. That is the way I used to think.

Now, in the new order of thinking, I shall endeavor to mentally see myself as keeping my appointment, etc.

I shall get into the spirit of the thought that nothing can impede my progress or thwart my purpose, and I am sure that a way will open enabling me to materialize this thought on the physical plane.

I am sure that in some unforeseen way my engagement will be kept, satisfactorily to myself and to the other person. In fact, I have experienced similar episodes.

Sage: Yes, almost everyone has had such experiences as you have related, but very few profit by them.

The law is, "As a man thinks so it becomes." If you wish to withdraw from an undesirable situation, you must adopt the scientific method of affirmative thinking, and follow it up as a permanent factor in life.

You will find that the universal causative Power (call it what you will) always manifests as supreme Intelligence in the adaptation of means to ends.

For instance, there is something which you wish to do – build a house, sell something, or do a kind act for someone.

It is this supreme Intelligence manifested through you that guides your activities. Without it, you would be unable to outline your intention, much less accomplish your purpose.

Your intelligence is the instrument through which the One Great Intelligence of the universe is constantly taking specific form.

This being true, every idea which registers in your mind was first formed in this One Infinite Mind. A continual recognition of this fact will enable you to find your way out of any sense of limitation which may arise in your individual experience.

I once heard of a man who had an intense desire to do big things. He asked his teacher to think with him along the lines just discussed –that the Intelligence of the universe was taking specific form in his individual intelligence.

His teacher agreed providing the student's desire was great enough to force him to arise every morning and take a two- mile walk, meanwhile meditating upon this interaction between the Universal Intelligence and its special form, his mind.

The student also was instructed to form the practice of making mental pictures for the precise purpose of developing his intuition and imagination.

One suggestion was that he should mentally see himself walking along a beautiful, clear, flowing river, hearing the rippling water, and seeing the reflection of the trees on its clear surface, and then to transfer his mental picture to one depicting his own desire.

After following this practice for six months, an idea of almost overwhelming magnitude came to his mind.

This did not seem unnatural, however, as it was so completely in accord with his recent habit of picturing his all absorbing desire.

He joyously continued his walks, his meditation, and visualization, and finally the Universal Intelligence manifested in its specific form (his mind) by giving specific directions to bring the big idea into successful operation.

Pupil: Could his mind have captured this big idea without the help of a teacher?

Sage: Certainly. The idea did not come through the teacher's mind; he simply started the student on the right track.

No one can think for another.

It was the result of his determined effort to recognize his own individual intelligence as the instrument in which the Greater Intelligence was constantly taking form.

All that the teacher did (all that anyone could do) was to help him to hold his thought along the path he desired to go.

The help of the teacher strengthened his conviction and faith in the power in himself.

Pupil: Is this originating power of life a forming power as well as a creating and direction one, and did the teacher's thinking along the same lines steady the student's thoughts?

Without the support of a more advanced mind, could anyone succeed in a great undertaking?

Sage: Certainly. If you are sufficiently convinced of the absolute truth of your method, you do not need any sustaining force outside of your own conviction. You miss the point of your relationship to the great whole if you do not realize that it is not only an originating, but also a forming power.

Do you not recognize its forming power throughout nature? You would not think of trying to make a lily a rose. If you know that the same Power that created the flowers also made your mind for the specific purpose of operating in it, you would soon learn to trust its formative nature in its operation through your intelligence.

Pupil: I understand.

It is the power of Life in man which originates, creates, directs, and forms.

In reality, there seems to be nothing whatever for man to do in this great scheme of things except to enjoy life, if he can only learn how!

God and Company, Ltd.

Sage: The Law of Life is God and Company. You are the Company, and you cannot in any sense be an idle partner, if you wish to profit by the partnership.

Your part is a big one, and there is plenty for you to do in providing a concrete center around which the universal divine energies can operate.

Pupil: Does this mean that to realize my oneness with the joy of life I shall not find it as simple as it seems?

Sage: No doubt there will be times when you will find it difficult to transfer your thought from externals to the interior realm of the originating principle and to joyfully hold it there until external conditions correspond with the ideas you have in mind, but there should never be any strain.

You are attracted to the Universal Mind as your source of supply, along the lines of least resistance.

That is to say, along these lines which are the most natural to your individual and particular bent of mind.

In this way you infuse into the Universal Mind your desires and ambitions, thus intensifying your power of attraction (relative to the desire uppermost in your mind) from the infinite forces.

For instance, let us suppose that you feel very much alone, not altogether lonely, but alone (there is a difference, you know), and yearn for congenial companionship.

At a certain night and morning, go where you will not be interrupted, and mentally picture yourself walking with a companionable friend (no person whom you know, but an ideal one); then see yourself riding with this same friend, and the two of you doing many happy things together.

Keep your picture in mind until all sense of aloneness has disappeared, and you feel an unmistakable sense of companionship.

Let that feeling register in your consciousness, and try to recall it at will.

If you will practice in this way, you will very soon realize that this is the reciprocal action between your mind and the Universal Mind.

Once this recognition is well established, your ideals will begin to express themselves in form.

Pupil: Then one's efforts should be wholly directed to the attainment of a higher degree of intelligence, rather than to the acquiring of material things?

"God Will Provide the Food, but He Will Not Cook the Dinner"

Sage: Such a purpose is the very highest, and aspirations along this line would surely externalize corresponding things.

Under no circumstances should you allow yourself to form the habit of idle dreaming. The material side of life should not be despised, for it is the outside of a corresponding inside, and has its place.

The thing to guard against is the acquiring of material possessions as your ultimate aim.

However, when certain external facts appear in the circle of your life, you should work with them diligently and with common sense.

Remember that things are symbols, and that the thing symbolized is more important than the symbol itself. "God will provide the food, but He will not cook the dinner."

Pupil: My part then is to cook the dinner, so to speak; to use the intelligence with which I have been endowed, by making it a power to attract, from out the universe, ideas that will provide for me in any direction that I may choose to go, according to law?

Sage: Yes, if you choose to go with life's continual, harmonious movement, you will find that the more you use the law of harmony through progressive thinking, the more intimately acquainted you will become with the law of reciprocity.

This law corresponds to the same principles which govern physical science; that is, "nature obeys you precisely in the same degree as you obey nature.

"This knowledge always leads to liberty".

Pupil: How does nature obey me?

Sage: Nature's first and greatest law is harmony.

You see the results of harmonious law in the beautiful world around you.

If you obey nature's suggestion, and follow the law you will be the recipient of all the benefits contained in this law of harmony that nature has to offer, such as health, strength, contentment, etc., for all of her laws bring freedom and harmony.

You will find nature responding along the same lines, to the extent that your thoughts and acts are in accordance with her perfect laws.

Pupil: Is the power of thought always creative, and does it always create conditions corresponding to itself? Can one know this law sufficiently well to cause it to respond immediately?

Fifteen Minutes Night and Day are Not Enough

Sage: Thought as thought is always creative, either good or bad.

The length of time required for the corresponding physical conditions to appear in the circle of your individual environment depends entirely upon your ability to recognize that your desired course is a normal, already existing, mental fact.

It is not enough to get into the spirit of your reasoning for fifteen minutes night and morning, with the inward confidence that you are directing a certain, unfailing power toward a desired physical manifestation, and then spend the remainder of your waking moments in doubt and fear.

The whole question is, how does your particular sustained thought affect you?

If it stimulates your feeling of faith, the response is immediate.

Pupil: Could you give me something to memorize which will help me to eliminate doubt and fear?

Sage: Yes. The thought I use most frequently myself is this: "My mind is a center of divine operation.

The divine operation is always for expansion and fuller expression, and this means the production of something beyond what has gone before, something entirely new, not included in past experience, though proceeding out of it by an orderly sequence of growth.

Therefore, since the divine cannot change the inherent nature, it must operate in the same manner in me: consequently, in my own special world, of which I am the center, it will move forward to produce new conditions always in advance of any that have gone before." (Dore Lectures)

You should memorize this passage and meditate upon it, endeavoring to make your mind a "center of divine operation," by entertaining only such thoughts as you feel are reflections of God's thoughts.

Whenever you sense that your way to freedom is obstructed, make a stronger endeavor to live with the spirit of your affirmation, and you will soon find your mind receiving ideas, which, if followed, will guide you into the path of absolute liberty.

The Devils of Doubt and Fear

Pupil: Doubt and fear are the devil, are they not?

Is not fear the more destructive of all wrong elements?

It seems to me that it is every present in one form or another. Can this monster be entirely eliminated from one's mind?

Sage: Surely. Although fear is the most destructive of all the mental enemies, and, as you say, seems to be ever present, yet when you realize that your fear is just as certain to materialize as is your faith, you will grow more and more guarded as to the quality of thought which you harbor.

Practice makes perfect.

Pupil: Try as I will to inhibit fear, I am unable to succeed at present. At times I utterly fail, and I am overwhelmed with it.

How to Drive Out Fear

Sage: The moment you begin to feel fearful, get into the open if possible, walk briskly for a mile or two, taking deep breaths, and holding your chin in and chest up.

Think of yourself as a monarch of all you survey and assume a corresponding commanding attitude.

Repeat with every breath this affirmation: "I am breathing in the Life, the Love, and the Power of the universe RIGHT NOW!"

Hold the breath a second, with the affirmation in the center of your mind; then expel the breath with the same thought and send it out to mingle with the ether of the universe. "I and my Father of Love are ONE."

If you cannot get out into the open, assume, wherever you are, the same attitude.

Take deep breaths, repeat the affirmation, and you feel certain that you are protected and supplied with all the love and power which Life has to give, fear will disappear, and you can resume whatever you were doing.

Strengthening Your Will

"All we have willed or hoped or dreamed of good, shall exist; Not its semblance, but itself; no beauty, nor good, nor power Whose voice has gone forth, but each survives for the melodist, When eternity affirms the conception of an hour."

Browning

Sage: The importance of the will is so frequently misunderstood that I think we will consider its true nature and purpose for a while this morning.

Almost everyone is conscious that willing is not imagining. What the function of the will is, for the most part, baffles and escapes our reasoning.

Pupil: I understand that most schools of mental science teach that one should not try to use or even understand the will, because to make conscious use of will-power leads one astray.

Sage: It is most important that you should have sufficient knowledge of your will not to misuse it, or to be led astray through lack of understanding its place and power.

Pupil: It is a compelling, creative power?

Sage: Correctly speaking, the will is neither one. It is in no sense creative. There are times, however, when a strong will can compel certain external combinations.

Pupil: If will-power can produce certain external results, why not use it to that end?

Sage: Because it was not intended to be used in this way.

Conditions brought into existence by mere force of will lack vitality; consequently, the situations brought about by simple will power disappear as soon as the will relaxes.

Pupil: Do the things which are forced into being through the power of a strong will disappear simply because they lack vitality, or because the compelling power relinquishes its hold?

Sage: Both, because of the lack of any real life in them, and because the energy of the will which supports them is withdrawn.

Pupil: I have read a great deal about the function of the will. What does it mean?

The Action or Function of the Will

Sage: It depends upon what you have read about the different kinds of will.

The will is the power-control in your mind, which holds your thought in a given direction until a result has been accomplished.

For example: Suppose you wish to go to a certain place; without the will to go there, you could not even start, nor could you retain the thought of the place long enough to arrive. You would start in the right direction, and then, because there was not sustaining power in the thought, you might turn and go in another direction.

Pupil: So it is the will which holds the thought to a given purpose until it is consummated; or keeps an idea in its place in one's mind until it is objectified in form.

It might be termed a thought-stabilizer.

Sage: Just so. It is the will which holds your mental faculties in position relative to the creative power which does the desired work.

Thought is always creative, as I have explained in my book "The Edinburgh Lectures of Mental Science," page 84:

"If, using the word in its widest sense, we may say that the imagination is the creative function, we may call the will the centralizing principle, its function being to keep the imagination centered in the right direction."

The will has much the same place in our mental machinery that the tool-holder has in a power-lathe. To my mind this is the will.

Pupil: It is a wonderfully clear statement. It means that success or failure is contingent upon but one thing: mental control, and the will is this controlling factor.

Sage: The business of the will is always the same, that of keeping your mental faculties where they will do the work you intend them to do.

Pupil: Suppose I were conducting a business, but my thoughts were more on an anticipated vacation than on my work. Naturally my business would suffer. How could my will help me?

Practice "Will Exercises"

Sage: The case you relate illustrates a weak will. You know that your thoughts should be kept on your business, but your will is too weak to do it.

You should practice will exercises to strengthen your mental energies. These will help you to focus your attention on business or any desired activity.

Pupil: If one concentrated his entire attention on business during business hours, would he be able to relax it later and enjoy his home and play?

Sage: With a properly trained will, you can pick up a thought at choice, hold it until it has finished its work, let it go again, and then pick up another thought, repeating the process again and again if you choose. In short, you can work when you work and play when you play.

Pupil: No doubt it can be done, but it seems to me now that it would be a terrible strain.

Sage: On the contrary, the well-trained, developed will maintains any position you desire without any strain on the nervous system, and its use is never followed by a sense of fatigue.

Pupil: I have always found it a great strain to hold on to any thought which did not abide in consciousness naturally.

Sage: This is an indication of a weak will, which should be strengthened through exercise, the beginning of which should be "a calm, peaceful determination to retain a certain mental attitude in spite of all temptations to the contrary, knowing that by doing so, the desired result will surely appear."

Pupil: Is the will intelligent?

"A Developed Will is the Handmaid of Intelligence"

Sage: The developed will is the handmaid of Intelligence. Pupil: What do you mean by that?

Sage: In training your will, you will become conscious of the presence of a tremendous power which acts on the plans of the very beginning, or first cause, of every so-called physical thing.

This power is the primary Living Intelligence of the universe.

Tell yourself what you desire in a clear, concise way, confidently knowing that it is certain to externalize itself as an objective fact, because your will acts upon the unformed creative, or primary, Intelligence, and causes it to take the form that you have determined upon.

Pupil: That does not sound so difficult. Of one thing I am certain, that is, that my entire environment is the result of my habitual tendency of thought.

Also, that when I know that I should turn my thoughts into other channels, but do not, simply letting them run along the lines of least resistance, it is because my will is weak and untrained. Will you please tell me the quickest way that this can be remedied?

Sage: I will give you a few exercises for developing the will, and from these you can fashion others to suit your own requirements.

In the first place, it is important to realize that any tendency to strain will be detrimental and must be avoided.

Such exercises are not only interesting, but stimulating, and if persistently practiced will keep your ambitions from lagging.

They will give you new impulses, renewed energy, and determination to be and to something better and greater than anything in the past.

Once you are fully conscious of the place and power of your will, in the mental realm, to keep the creative energy at work in formulating your desires, you will realize that it is very susceptible to training, and you will never again be content to live without its constant use, for it would be like living only half a life.

Pupil: May I ask a question right here? I am a fairly good pianist but dislike to begin my practice, and, although I enjoy it once I have begun, to start is always a struggle.

If I were to compel myself to practice on the piano at a certain time every day, would that develop and strengthen my will?

Sage: It would help, but the greatest benefit would be in the direction of making you a better musician.

The best way to strengthen your will is to practice exercises for the sole purpose of strengthening the will, always remembering, while taking them, that your effort is for self- training and self-control, to the end that you many realize yourself as a part of the great universal whole.

In this way you gain a peaceful centralization, which, though maintained by a conscious act of the will, is the very essence of rest.

With a well-developed, trained will, your thoughts will never wander from the consciousness that "all is life, and all is good, and nature, from her clearly visible surface to her most arcane depths, is a storehouse for good."

You have the key to her great treasures, and whatever appeals to you most at any particular time and place, is that mode of the universal Living Spirit with which you are at that moment most in touch.

Realizing this, you draw from out the universe streams of vital energy, which make the very act of living a joy, which radiate from you vibrations that can turn aside all injurious suggestions.

This is surely a good and sufficient reason for developing the will.

Exercise for Strengthening the Will

The will is weak because of lack of exercise. Training the will is very much the same as training the muscles.

Its development is gradual. Only will can develop will; consequently, you begin with what will you have, and expand and strengthen it thought its action upon itself.

The weak will manifests in two phases: over-action and under-action; the former as impulsiveness, impetuousness, and the life, and the latter as lethargy, phlegmatism, etc.

It is good to begin each day with a resolution not to hurry, and not to leave any task unfinished.

Effort in this direction is of inestimable value. There should be only one object in your mind with reference to your exercise –the development and strengthening of your will.

At the time have no thought of your improvement as a musician, for if there is any ulterior motive, your will- training will be lost sight of.

Cultivate the Feeling of Contentment

Cultivate the sense of contentment, and begin your exercise with that feeling, determining to do it in a happy frame of mind. This is important.

Take your exercise at a time of day when interruptions are least likely to occur, for 7 consecutive days, 10 consecutive minutes a day.

If an interruption occurs during the exercise, start all over again.

If you forget the exercise for one day before you have finished your course of 7 days, begin the entire set again and go through with it uninterruptedly.

Place a notebook and pencil by your side before beginning. Now take fifty matches, beads, buttons, bits of paper, or any other small objects, and drop them slowly and deliberately into a box one by one, with a feeling of contentment and satisfaction, declaring with each movement, "I will to will."

The one and most important thought is that you are training your will for the particular advantage of having a trained will, and this is why you should cultivate the feeling of contentment.

The only method by which you can study the development of your will is by self-analysis and introspection, so, when you have finished your practice, ask yourself such questions as these:

"What did I think about the exercise while I was doing it? Did I believe it would really cultivate my will, or did I do it just because I was told to?

Did I actually concentrate on dropping the matches into the box, or was I more concerned with their arrangement, or was I distracted with other thoughts, good or bad?

Was I watching the time impatiently, or was I consciously engaging in thoughts of satisfaction and contentment?

Did I have a sense of strain, or did it brace me up?

Do I believe that it will really train my will if I faithfully follow it up long enough to prove it?" etc., etc.

Write down this series of questions and answers in your notebook. You will find it both interesting and encouraging to keep this record and thus watch your progress.

Stimulating an Interest in Your Will Exercise

You can stimulate interest in your exercise by varying your resolution or intention.

That is, one time hold a conscious attitude of joyously willing to will, another of powerfully willing to will, another of peacefully, and another contentedly, etc., etc.

These variations in the exercise with the suggestions for introspection, which have been slightly changed, were taken from the best authority, as far as I know, along the lines of will-training, and I am positive will bring the attainment of a firm, strong will, and an intelligent use of it.

Lesson V

Making Your Subjective Mind Work for You

"The most potent force in the universe is the influence of the subconscious mind. The proper training of the correlation between the subliminal and the objective faculties is the open sesame that unlocks the richest of all storehouses, -- the faculty of remembering. And with remembering there follows natural reflections, vision, knowledge, culture, and all that tends to make of man a God, though in the germ."

– Dr. Edwin F. Bowers

Pupil: The subject of the subjective mind greatly interests me.

I am sure that had I understood what you have said concerning it, I would have realized that all that was necessary to obtain my desires was to think out exactly what I wanted, consciously place it in my subjective mind, and it would at once begin to attract ways and means for its corresponding physical or material fulfillment.

Sage: Indeed the study of the subjective mind is an all- absorbing subject.

I may be able to enlighten and help you to make working realities out of what now seems to be vague and even mysterious.

But it will rest entirely with you to put vitality into these suggestions, and that can only be accomplished through using them.

Pupil: You mean that by making practical use of your suggestions, I will be able to attain practical results which will help not only myself but others also?

Sage: That is the idea. It has always seemed to me that the average person prefers the satisfaction of giving to another what he requires, rather than helping or teaching him how to attract the desired things to himself, which would give him in addition a feeling of assurance and liberty.

You would unquestionably enjoy giving to others, and the recipient would likewise enjoy receiving, but, as a rule, it tends to pauperize the spirit of independence.

Pupil: If I were to put into my subconscious mind a definite idea that all people have the same power in their subconscious minds to attract to themselves the things they desire through their own efforts, would that thought register in their subconscious minds?

Sage: That would be the intelligent way of impersonally helping others to connect with their limitless supply.

Pupil: You have told me before that there was a definite way of impressing the subconscious mind with a particular thought.

Would you mind explaining this again?

"Get into the Spirit of Your Desire"

Sage: The process is quite different from that of retaining an idea in the so-called intellectual mind. It is necessary, above all else, to get into the spirit of your desire, and an effort to feel relaxed and confident will help you to do this.

"The spirit of a thing is that which is the source of its inherent movement."

For example, if you wish to impress your subconscious mind with the sense of contentment, you must meditate on the quality of contentment. See how that affects you.

If in response to your meditation you feel relaxed and confident, you may be sure that your subconscious mind has been impressed with that thought.

This is getting "into the spirit" of contentment; not because of certain physical reasons, but because of your recognition of life's action in you in this specific direction.

You have the whole of Universal Mind to draw from. There is no limit to the creative power of your subjective mind once you have impressed it with your intention. This example applies to everything great or small.

Pupil: Since my subjective mind is a part of the Universal Mind, if I impress it with an idea or desire, does this impression pass automatically into the Universal Subjective Mind?

Sage: Your subjective mind is in essence the same as the Universal Subjective Mind with which it is inseparably connected.

It should be understood that your subjective mind receives its impressions from the objective mind and never from material things.

It is therefore necessary to withdraw your thought from the material or physical thing you desire, and to mentally dwell upon the spiritual symbol of it, which is the inherent source of its formation.

How to Visualize and Objectify the Mental Image

All this may seem somewhat involved to you, because it is the study of the intangible rather than the tangible, but it will unfold to you as we go on, and it will seem quite simple.

All we know of the invisible is gained from what we see it do on the plane of the visible.

Perhaps an illustration will give you a clearer idea of that interior part of your being, which is the support of all that which must naturally subsist in the universal here and the everlasting now.

First, endeavor to realize yourself as pure spirit, the essential quality of which is good.

Pure spirit is pure life, and naturally, the only thing it could desire is to manifest more and more life, without reference to the forms through which the manifestation takes place.

Consequently, "the purer your intention, the more readily it is placed in your subconscious mind," which instantly passes it into the Universal Mind.

For example: If you want a house, a certain kind of a chair, a sum of money, or anything else, you should first ponder studiously on how the desired object originated.

Meditating thus on the original spirit of the thing in question starts the creative power of your subjective mind (which is in touch with all the creative energy which exists) operating in that specific direction.

Suppose it is a house you desire.

You will go back to the original concept of it.

The idea of a house had its origin in a primary need for shelter, protection from the elements, and comfort, and out of these original desires there grew our present dwellings.

So you proceed to build a house in your own consciousness first, thinking only harmonious, constructive thoughts regarding it.

This kind of thinking (or building) gives your subjective mind definite material to work with, and because of its amenableness to suggestion, coupled with its native creative power, it will go ahead and eventually bring the house into manifestation.

> Pupil: If I earnestly and righteously desire a certain kind of a home, how shall I proceed?

> Sage: You should first form a clear conception in your objective mind of the sort of a house which you desire; whether one, two, or three stories; the number and size of the rooms; how many windows and doors; in short, you should mentally picture the completed house, both inside and out.

> Go all around the house; look over the exterior; then go indoors and examine it carefully from cellar to garret in every detail.

> Then drop the picture and dwell in the spiritual prototype of the house.

> Pupil: I do not fully understand what the spiritual prototype is?

> Sage: The simplest method of finding a spiritual prototype of any object is to ask yourself to what use it is to be put, what does it stand for, in other words, what is the reason for its being?

> As we have been saying, a house is a place of shelter, comfort, protection. It might be called a refuge.

Pupil: Then if I want a house (really a home), and there seems no ordinary way of my having it, I am to impress my desire upon by subjective mind, by mentally picturing the type of house I want, in conjunction with the ideas of shelter, comfort, and protection, and mentally live in that state of mind, while, in order to supplement a mental atmosphere of "pure intention," I admit no thoughts of discord, such as anger, jealousy, doubt, fear, etc., but entertain thoughts of love, joy, beauty, and harmony.

Would this not be literally living in my true mental abode. And could I not expect to see it objectified in a material home?

Sage: Yes, because every physical or material thing is the result of an idea first possessed in consciousness.

These ideas, which are universal by nature, are specialized by your mental picture, and your concentrated effort to inhibit thoughts which concern the operation of the laws of life.

This habit of thought-formation, if persisted in, opens the way for the physical manifestation of the mental picture, whatever it may be, the case in point being a house.

A house is an effect of a need for shelter, comfort, protection, and the like.

Pupil: I have never thought before of what a house really symbolized.

It seems quite natural now to think of it as an externalized object of an inward originating idea of comfort, shelter, and protection, which you have taught me is its prototype.

Now, my natural impulse would be to go into the house and bolt the doors and windows, if I were afraid of some outside invasion and wanted to protect myself.

Yet this might not always give me a feeling of security. From where does that sense of real protection come?

Living in the Sense of Protection

Sage: The first necessity would be for you to have the house to go into, before you could bolt the doors and windows against unwelcome intrusion or impending danger.

After having acquired this refuge, it alone would not insure complete protection.

The feeling of protection is established within yourself through your knowledge that you are protected by the Almighty, Ever-Present, Intelligent Power of Life.

Surely you know you are alive, and this understanding brings a sense of security which locked doors or barred windows cannot give.

Pupil: It would be wonderful if one could constantly live in that thought of protection!

Sage: It is to this end we are journeying. As we have seen, in the mind of man there is a power which enables him to contact the unlimited universal Power of God, Spirit, and thereby envelop himself in it.

One of the most satisfying and comforting feelings possible is this one of being protected from within oneself.

Pupil: I see. One should endeavor to keep the suggestion of one's real self, which is one's real protection, constantly in mind; that self which is one with all Life and all Intelligence, which not only preserves but provides for all.

To return to the subject of the house.

It being, then, the outward fulfillment or manifestation of a desire or need for shelter and protection, the mode of procedure necessary to procure it would be to get into the spirit of Life's intelligent protection, and it in turn would attract the necessary conditions to bring into tangible being a house, or whatever form of refuge was most required, and visualized?

Sage: Mentally entering into the spirit of Life's amenable creative force, it will take any special form your desire gives it, which is mentally pictured or visualized.

The house is only an illustration.

Pupil: I understand. Now suppose one wanted more money or better health.

What would be the prototype for these?

Sage: It is always best to find one's own prototype. Let us refer to the suggestions I have already given you.

What does money symbolize? For what is it to be used? For myself, I find that the prototype for money is Substance, and my method for manifesting more money is to mentally picture the sum I require for a particular purpose, either in bank-notes, check, or draft, whichever seems the most natural.

After making a clear, distinct picture, I enlarge my vision of money as the symbol of life's substance, as applied to the use I intend to put it to.

I believe that money is the greatest factor for constructive exchange that we have today.

How to Develop Health and Harmony

In the case of money, you would hold firmly in your mind the fact that the Substance of Life fills all space.

It is, indeed, the starting point of all things, whether it takes the form of desired sums of money or of something else.

For physical health you would endeavor to keep your thought as harmonious as possible, and mentally picture yourself as well and doing the useful, happy things in your daily life that a healthy person would naturally do, always understanding that the originating Life Principle in you must act harmoniously upon itself in order to produce harmonious physical results.

Pupil: Then the most important point in demonstrating health is not so much the mental picture, as the control of thought in a definite center, irrespective of conditions or symptoms –really living in the prototype, a wholly perfect and harmonious expression of God the Father Spirit, the source of health and life?

Sage: Exactly, and this is where your trained will comes in to help you to hold your picture and to steadfastly live in your prototype.

The mental picture is the seed you plant, so to speak, and the quality of thought which you entertain most persistently impresses itself upon the subconscious mind and starts the creative energy molding itself into the form of your mental picture.

Pupil: Then Life's only creative power is Subjective Mind, which reproduces on the outward or physical plane the idea with which it has been impressed.

What a field of possibilities this stupendous fact opens up if one could only prove it!

Sage: To obtain continuous good results it is a necessity to properly understand your relation to this great unformed, highly impressionable power you are dealing with.

"Never try to make yourself believe what you know is not true."

Unless your faith is built upon the solid foundation of absolute conviction, you will never be able to make practical use of it.

Pupil: This solid foundation of conviction, –how can it be established permanently? One day I feel sure of it, and the next my assurance seems to have turned to stone, and nothing I can do will bring it to life again!

Sage: You give your unqualified consent that you possess this creative power when you use it constructively instead of destructively.

Remember, that the creative energy has only one method of operating, which is its reciprocal action from the Universal Mind to your subjective mind, and then from your subjective mind back into the Universal Subjective Mind which is its source, and which unfailingly corresponds to the thought which originally generated it.

Your greatest aim should be to irrevocably convince yourself that the Originating Spirit which brought the whole world into existence is the root of your individuality.Therefore, it is "ever ready to continue its creative action through you."

Just as soon and just as fast as you provide these thought channels, you will find yourself the possessor of an unfailing reproductive power.

Pupil: I suppose I am not unlike others, in that I am always willing to take all the credit for the good which comes to me, and unwilling to take the credit for my miseries, placing the blame on somebody or some condition over which I believe I have no control.

How can I overcome this wretched tendency?

Sage: I can only repeat, by endeavoring steadfastly to remember that the only creative power there is has but one way of working, which is that of reciprocal action.

There is only one primary cause; the Universal Subjective Mind, of which your own subjective mind is a part. To gain in understanding, it is necessary to be persistent in impressing your subconscious mind with the fact of its relationship to the unlimited whole.

Bring your every thought and feeling into obedient connection with the best there is in you.

This old saying has a world of truth in it:

"What thou see'st, that thou be'st; dust if thou see'st dust; God if thou see'st God."

Hold the Thought of What You Are, to Guide You into What You Want to Be.

Pupil: Which means, I suppose, that the law is always the same.

The thought I maintain becomes a fact in my mental as well as in my physical plane, so I must hold the thought of what

I really am in order to become what I would like to be?

Sage: Yes, endeavor never to lose sight of this fact.

Pupil: Like the illustration you gave of the house, it has its birth in the idea of protection, irrespective of any physical form?

Sage: Protection is an inherent quality of life; consequently it fills all space, ever ready to be called into any form of expression.

If you get into the spirit of that idea, you will see how quickly corresponding results will appear. Because the quality of the subject mind is the same in you as it is "throughout the universe, giving rise to the multitude of natural forms with which you are surrounded, also giving rise to yourself."

It really is the supporter of your individuality.

Your individual subjective mind is your part in the great whole, as I have declared before. The realization of this will enable you to produce physical results through the power of your own thought.

Pupil: That reveals to me your meaning in "The Edinburgh Lectures" where you say, "One should regard his individual subjective mind as the organ of the absolute, and his objective mind as the organ of the relative."

I will never forget that fact again.

Cultivate the Idea of Protection

Sage: The idea in the absolute is the very beginning (or nucleus) of the thing, regardless of the form through which it expresses.

For instance, the pure idea of protection exists in life itself (is one of its innate qualities) and has no relation to a house or any building erected for that purpose.

Pupil: Then it is my objective mind or intellect which suggests to this self-existing, absolute power the idea of this relationship?

Sage: Quite so, and if you will pattern the thought you have just expressed, telling your subconscious mind over and over again that it is the one and only creative power, which always brings into physical manifestation corresponding forms of the ideas with which it is impressed, you will realize the joys of success.

Pupil: I "see through a glass darkly."

Is there no way to develop a keener sense of just how to awaken the subconscious mind so that it will respond more quickly?

Sage: I will be happy to give you a copy of a letter I once wrote in response to a question similar to yours.

This letter was considered so helpful that the men to whom it was written had it put into pamphlet form, now out of print.

It seems to me that the main thing that I said in that letter was "Don't try!"

Pupil: Why! I thought that trying was to be my main endeavor, even though it was difficult?

A Letter of Golden Leaves

The Sage's Letter

"To answer your question as to how a "Keener sense of the subjective mind may be awakened," the answer is 'Don't try. Don't try to make things what they are not.'

Subjective mind is subjective just because it lies below the threshold of consciousness.

It is the Builder of the Body, but we can neither see, hear, nor feel it building.

Just keep in your conscious mind a quiet, calm expectation that subjective mind is always at work in accordance with the habitual thought of your objective mind...and then subjective mind will take care of itself.

Then the question is, how to keep the conscious thought in a life –enjoying and life-giving current.

My answer to this is very simple, thought perhaps old- fashioned.

It is, keep looking at God. Don't trouble about theology, but try to realize the Universal Divine Spirit as perpetually flowing through all things; through insensible things as atomic energy; through animals as instinct; through man as thought.

If this be so, then your manifestation of God will correspond with your habitual thought of God.

Quietly contemplate the Divine Spirit as a continual flowing of Life, Light, Intelligence, Love and Power, and you will find this current flowing through you and manifesting in a hundred ways, both mentally and physically, in your affairs.

You do not make this current, but you prepare the conditions which will either cause it to trickle through thinly and weakly, or flow through strongly.

You prepare the conditions on the interior side by a mental attitude of looking into the light (God is Light) with the expectancy of thence receiving life and Illumination, and on the exterior side by not denying in your work what you are trying to hold in your thought, –for yourself the simple Law of Enjoyment of all that you can enjoy, ruled by moderation, and toward others equally the simple Law of Honesty and Kindness.

I know you have heard these things ever since you were a child, but what we all want is to realize our connection with the building power within.

The connection is this: that the Spirit, as it flows through you, becomes you, and it becomes in you just what you take it for, just as water takes the shape of the pipe it flows through.

It takes shape from your thought. It is exceedingly sensitive –how much more, then, must the pure Life Principle itself be sensitive? Think over this. Think it over and then think.

Think of it kindly, lovingly, trustfully, and as a welcome companion. It will respond exactly.

Think of it as a Living Light, continually flowing through and vivifying you, and it will respond exactly.

If you ask why it does this, the answer is because IT is the Infinite of your Real Self.

Let this answer suffice you. You will only darken the Light by trying to analyze the Divine Spirit. You cannot dissect God. This doesn't mean being impractical, but getting to the very root of truly practical.

We have our ordinary business to do, but, believe me, it is the scientific method to bring everything into the Divine Light.

Then let your ideas be desires to see it in the Divine Light, let your ideas regarding it grow quietly of themselves, and you will see it in its proper and true light whatever the thing may be.

Then when you have seen what the thing really is, go on and handle it in accordance with the four principles of Cheerfulness, Moderation, Honestly and Kindness.

Don't worry, and don't try to force things; let them grow, because, by recognizing the continual flow of the Spirit, you are providing the conditions, for Life is the Light which will make them grow the right way.

Don't bother about subjective mind and objective mind, or theories of any sort, or description, either mine or anyone else's; but just do what I have said and try it for six months, and I think you will find you have got hold of the Power that Works, and, after all, that is what we want.

It is all summed up in this: Live naturally with the Spirit and don't worry.

Remember, you and your Spirit are One, and it is all quite natural. You will perhaps say that this is too simple.

Well, we don't want to introduce unnecessary complications. Try practicing and leave the theory to take care of itself.

"Living Spirit is not to be found in a book."

Sage: Many have written me from all parts of the world voicing your expression.

Once a lady in New York City wrote asking me to explain to her exactly what I mean in the pamphlet about Spirit becoming you.

Thinking you might like to see a copy of my reply, I brought it along for you.

Pupil: Thank you so much. Am I at liberty to keep these letters?

Sage: Quite.

The Letter of the Master

With regard to the sentence in the pamphlet on the Subjective Mind about the Spirit becoming you, I really don't see how to express my meaning any more clearly.

What I mean is that in a cat it becomes a cat; and in a cabbage it becomes a cabbage; but in man, who is conscious, living intelligence, it becomes conscious, living intelligence.

And if so, then since the Spirit is Infinite you can by prayer and meditation draw upon it for increase living intelligence, i.e., all depends on your mode of recognition of it.

In the sentence you quote, 'It is exceedingly sensitive,' etc,. I am not referring to the water, but the Spirit.

I mean that if subconscious mind in ourselves is sensitive to suggestion, the creative principle is sensitive to suggestion, the creative principle from which it springs must be still more so, and takes shape from your thought accordingly.

But you must remember that the pamphlet was not written for publication. It was merely a private letter, and I was never consulted on the subject of publishing it, or perhaps I should have worded it more carefully.

Supply and demand is a very large subject, but eventually you will always have to come back to the teaching of Jesus, "Ask and ye shall receive."

We may write volumes on the subject, but in the end it always comes to this, and we have gained nothing by going a long way around.

I am coming more and more to see that the teaching of Jesus is the final embodiment of all that writers on those subjects are trying to teach.

In the end we have to drop all our paraphernalia of argument and come back to His statement of the working method.

All the Bible premises are based on the divine knowledge of your mental constitution, and by simple reliance on it we therefore afford centers through which the Creative Power of the Universe can act in correspondence with our recognition of it.

'According to your faith so be it unto you.' Our faith is our real thought. If our real thought is expectation of disease and poverty, and so open the door to it.

The whole purpose of the Bible is to direct our thought (which is our faith) in the right way, instead of leaving us to form it invertedly.

Therefore, as the basis for our faith, the Bible gives us Promises.

Pin your faith to the Promises, and you need not bother your brains to argue about it.

The more you argue, the more you will pin your faith to your own argument and your understanding of the law; and as a logical sequence you make the fulfillment of your desire depend on your correct arguing and exact knowledge, so that the result is you are depending entirely upon yourself – and so you are 'no forwarder' and are just simply where you were.

On the other hand by simply believing the Divine Promises, you transfer the whole operation to the Divine Spirit (your subjective mind), and so you have a good ground of expectation, and by your mental receptive attitude you become a 'fellow worker' with God.

You allow the All Creating Spirit to work in, for, and through you.

This is the conception St. Paul always had in his epistles, in all of them showing the weakness of relying on Law, and the strength of Faith in Promises.

This also, I think, was Jesus' meaning when He said:

'Blessed is he that hath not seen and yet hath believed.'

Well, I hope that these few remarks will be useful to you, but I am wondering how this point of view will appeal to an American audience, and that is another reason why I am rather doubtful about coming over.

The more I think of this subject, the less I see in trying to make 'Supply,' 'Health.' and all the usual New Thought topics the subject of a set of mechanical rules like the rules of arithmetic.

It throws the burden back on yourself, while your whole object is to get rid of it.

It is the old temptation of Eden over again —the Tree of Knowledge, reliance on our own acquisition of Knowledge; on the Tree of Life, —reliance of God's own nature and His desire for expression in us and through us, which is the meaning of all the promises.

The former looks clever but isn't. The latter looks childish but is the fulfillment of all law, and is life.

If you see things in this light, which I am sure is the true one, the model you will have to take for the 'School of the Builders' is 'The stone which the builders rejected has become the head of the corner.'

The reference is to the great pyramid and the topmost stone —also to our crowning stone in Westminster Abbey —and of course it refers superlatively to Christ.

But properly instructed builders do not reject this stone. On the contrary, they recognize it as both the Foundation and the apex of the Building of the Temple.

You remember how St. Paul calls himself a wise master- builder.

Is it any use for me to come to America to teach these things, which is some form or another have been taught there ever since the arrival of the Mayflower?

Of course, I can talk about Vibration, Nervous System, the Pyramid, and the like, and the working of Natural Laws; but the Creating Principle is apart.

A worshipper of God and a student of Nature; is what one of our old thinkers called himself. The Power is of God and is received by Man and Man exercises it upon nature. That is the true order.

One meaning of the Masonic symbol of the five pointed star is that everything returns to its starting point.

Start from the apex of the triangle and trace the line around and you come back to the apex. If, then, your starting point is in Heaven, you go back to Heaven and the Divine Power, and so get rid of the burden; but if your starting point is on earth (i.e., your own acquisition of knowledge of laws), you get back to earth, which is indicated by the inverted triangle.

You will find the Promises of man's power over Nature, Conditions, etc., fully stated in Mark 11: 22-25, and no teaching can promise more than this."

God Has Ripened a Great Mind

Pupil: No words can express what a privilege I feel it to have you thus unfold and make clear to me the truths I have struggled so hard to understand.

God has surely blessed you with one of the greatest minds of the present generation.

Sage: Not at all. There are many who know much more than I along these lines.

For myself, however, I am certain that there is but one God, that God and man are one, and that my mind is a center of Divine Operation; this in itself is a blessing.

Much has already been written on these subjects; it is all so simple.

Sage: I am happy indeed that these lessons have been helpful. It has been a great pleasure for me to have exchanged ideas with you, and I know that you will pass them on to others whenever you feel they will be helpful.

It seems to me that you now have all the material necessary to build for yourself a foundation and superstructure of absolute faith in God and of the power of God in you, which is your subjective mind.

This knowledge, well established, gives you dominion over every adverse circumstance and condition, because you are in conscious touch with your limitless supply. "Only believe in the God within, and all things are possible unto you."

Pupil: I know it is simple to you, but to us, who are struggling between certainty and uncertainty, it is a rare benefit to be able to sit and listen at the feet of certainty.

Sage: I am happy indeed that these lessons have been helpful. It has been a great pleasure for me to have exchanged ideas with you, and I know that you will pass them on to others whenever you feel they will be helpful. It seems to me that you now have all the material necessary to build for yourself a foundation and superstructure of absolute faith in God and of the power of God in you, which is your subjective mind. This knowledge, well established, gives you dominion over every adverse circumstance and condition, because you are in conscious touch with your limitless supply. "Only believe in the God within, and all things are possible unto you."

Hourly Helps

Sage: I want in this lesson to give you, in the most practical form, the means whereby you may meet the disquieting things of life –the things which wear soul, spirit, and body almost to the snapping point.

I want you to take these admonitions and instructions into your most intimate life and keep them bright and shining by daily use.

They will help you hourly in overcoming destructive elements, and in attracting constructive ones.

Anger

When anger begins to stir you, take deep breaths; hold your thought on the inflow of breath as being rays of light, breathing deeper and deeper.

Continue the deep breaths until you have taken twenty-five inhalations; hold each one while you count to seven.

Then expel slowly, keeping your thought steadily on the inhalation, mentally seeing it go all through your lungs, and penetrating every part of your body's rays of light.

Then meditate upon any real live thought about yourself, such as being one with all life and good. A little practice in this way will soon relieve you of the tendency to anger.

Anxiety

When conditions are not to your liking and you find yourself thinking more and more about how unhappy you are because of them, stay out of doors in the open all you possibly can.

> Endeavor to walk at least two miles every day, breathing deeply of the fresh air with this thought: "I am breathing in the Life, the Love and the Power of the universe, right now."

Do not permit your thought to slip back into the old groove. Fill your mind with this declaration about yourself.

You have been given dominion over every adverse condition through your power of thought. Persist in your steady recognition of this fact.

Tell yourself over and over again that all is well right now in your thought and feeling; consequently outside conditions must and will correspond.

Disease

If your body is the expression of thought, then disease must be the result of a belief that your body is subject to disease.

Tell yourself many times a day that all physical disease is the result of discordant thoughts, and when you have actually accepted this statement as a truth, you will be careful to entertain only healthy, harmonious thoughts for yourself or another.

For example, if you feel a headache coming on, begin at once to take deep breaths, and repeat with each breath that breath is Life, and that life is perfect health.

"I am alive, so the health of life is manifesting in me right now."

Disappointment

This subtle destructive power should be shut out at all times by the recognition of your direct contact with all the joy there is, because you are one with its Source, Universal Good.

If the joyous life does not express itself through the exact channels which you expect, know that it will do so through others.

Life wants to express joy through you, for it made you an instrument in which and through which to do it. Because you are here for that purpose. You can and do enjoy all the good which Life has to give.

Take some physical exercises while holding that thought. A good one is to sit on a chair and take a deep breath; then slowly exhale, and as you exhale, gradually bend at the hips until you can touch the floor with the tips of your fingers. Repeat this seven times with the affirmation: "The joy of
God is flowing in me and through me right now."

Discontent

When this enemy to peace and happiness begins to advance, sing, sing, sing, right out loud if you can, or else do it mentally.

Sing anything you like.

Watch your breath control, and every night put into your subconscious mind the thought that God brought you into existence for the purpose of expressing all of Life's harmonies, both in you and through you, and it is your divine right to BE harmony and to be harmonious in your daily experience.

Meditate upon the harmony you see expressed in nature and endeavor to apply it in your thought, and then express it.

Discouragement

This is failure on your part to recognize the Almighty limitless Source of Supply (God) as your never-failing, co- operative partner.

When you are assailed with the thought of discouragement, immediately ask yourself, "What kind of a power was it that brought me into existence, and for what purpose?"

Then repeat slowly and thinkingly, "I do believe and I am persuaded that God is an ever-present, never-failing source of protection and supply."

Watch your thoughts lest any contrary to this affirmation be lurking around in the corners of your mind, and stick to it with all the will that you have, and you will break down the suggestion that there is any power in discouragement.

Envy

Envy is due to a sense of separation from God, Good. Endeavor to realize that where there is life, all that life has to give is present in its entirety at all times and in all places, and will come into visible expression through the persistent recognition of this grand fact.

Fear

One writer has said that fear is the only devil there is.

Certainly it is the most destructive power one can entertain.

When fear comes to assail you, close the door of your mind against it with this positive thought: "The only creative power there is, is thought.

All things are possible to him who believes that the God which brought man into existence did so for the purpose of expressing His Fatherly love and protection in His child.

I believe in God, the Father almighty, as my life, my intelligence, manifesting in my consciousness now." As you think this, walk briskly or take strenuous exercise. Whenever you sense fear returning, inhibit it instantly by substituting any thought which affirms the power of God in you.

In short, fear is absolutely overcome by withdrawing your thought from the physical reason or argument which would cause you to believe in a power other than God, and the spirit of Life and Love as your birthright.

Indecision

This is a lack of the realization that your intelligence is the instrument through which the Intelligence of the universe takes specific form.

An effort to realize this fact should be a habit of mind, rather than spasmodic attempts made only with the necessity for decision arises.

Jealousy

This is love's greatest enemy, and if permitted to dwell within your consciousness, will ultimately destroy your ability to enjoy your life.

It is the reaction of the fear of loss and can be overcome through prayer and watchfulness.

Reason along these lines:

"God is Life and God is Love. I am life and I am love.

I cannot lose Love any more than I can lose Life." When you are tempted to feel jealous, walk long distances as frequently as possible and keep your thought on Love itself, not on any one person whom you love, but just Love and its attributes.

Think of God as Love. Keep all thought of personality out of mind, and you will find that love will spring up in you as a fountain of everlasting love and life and fill your consciousness through and through.

Self-Condemnation

The instant you begin to blame yourself for having done the wrong thing or for not having done the right thing, put this thought into your consciousness to the exclusion of every other:

"Infinite Intelligence and Wisdom are expressing themselves in me more and more right now."

Take the exercise of bending the body from the hips (without bending the knees) so that you can touch the floor with the tips of your fingers, inhaling as you lift the body, and exhaling every time you bend.

Repeat this exercise sixteen times, accompanied by the affirmation just given.

Self-Indulgence

This is brought about by lack of will-power: an evidence of a weak will. It means failure, because you have no thought-power to give the unformed energy of life the particular thought-material necessary to produce desired results. Absolute mental (thought) control is the one and only thing which is necessary for you to do, to be, or to have what you want.

Without it, you scatter your forces. If you permit your thoughts to run riot without restraint, the conditions of your life will become chaotic.

For example: A friend does something of which you do not approve, or perhaps your present circumstances are undesirable. Refuse to let your thought dwell on the injustice of your friend, for dwelling on it would only produce greater unhappiness for you.

Control your thought and do not think of your friend in this connection. Instead, consider the many fine attributes of friendship, and this will restore harmony. Do the same in regard to your unpleasant circumstances.

Don't picture them mentally and say to yourself, "How dreadful they are!" But repeat the glorious truth which I have previously referred to:

"My mind is a center of divine operation." etc., and divine operation is always for greater advancement and better things.

You will experience this if you cling faithfully to this line of reasoning.

Sensitiveness

A highly sensitive mind is simply a "self-mind," a form of unadulterated selfishness.

Your feelings are hurt because someone says something which you do not like, or does something which displeases you. Or conversely, he fails to say or to do what you think he should.

To eradicate this baneful thought-habit, use the same method of argument as for self-indulgence, and if faithful in your mental work, your efforts will be rewarded, and you will free yourself.

Unhappiness

A continually unhappy state of mind is the direct result of constantly viewing life from the physical standpoint as though that were life's only reality.

Every night, before you go to sleep, put well into your subconscious mind this thought: "There is but One Mind to think about me or to make laws over me, and that is the Mind of Divine Love and Divine Power." Every morning meditate upon this thought.

Use it as your shield and buckler at the first suggestion of any sense of unhappiness.

You will soon find that the tendency to be discontented and unhappy will vanish, and happier conditions will come into your experience.

Lesson VII

Putting Your Lessons into Practice

Just as I am completing this manuscript for the printer, the idea suggests itself that it will also be helpful to give a definite idea, in formula form, of how to be and have what you want.

First, you should endeavor to learn to be as near the perfect reflection of your own idea of God as possible, in thought and action.

It may seem impossible at first thought, to even approach such a goal, but reflection upon the thought that God made you out of Himself, because He wished to see and feel Himself in you, will help you to persevere.

When you first began to learn to read, no doubt you felt in your childish way that it would be wonderful to read as well as the grown-ups could; you kept on trying and then you read.

Perhaps you have a big desire which you would give your life to have fulfilled.

In reality it is only necessary for you to give a few moments each day to earnest effort, in getting into the spirit of this idea of God and living in it every waking hour.

Then endeavor to find the Spiritual Prototype for your desire. By this I mean inhibit all thought of the physical side of your desire.

If you desire a true companion, close your mind entirely to all personality and physical being, and dwell in thought and feeling on the spirit of love and true comradeship, without reference to any physical person.

The person is the instrument through which these particular qualities manifest, and not the qualities themselves, as we often learn too late.

Or you may desire improved financial condition. Here again it is not mere money you desire. It is that which money symbolizes –Substance, Liberty, Freedom from lack.

Therefore, you should go alone night and morning (or any time when you are certain you will not be disturbed) and meditate first upon your own true relation to God.

After your feeling has been stimulated to the point of certainty, then meditate upon the ever-present, never- failing substance and freedom of God.

Try not to lose sight of the fact that the greatest magnet for acquiring money is Ideas. There is every reason that you should capture one of these big money ideas, if you will persistently follow the suggestions given.

If you do this, you will not only capture the idea, but also the courage to put the idea into practical application.

This courage, put to positive uses, will bring you to the goal of your desire-substance, love, friends, health, happiness, and the peace that passeth all understanding.

May all these come to you in richest measure.